CAPITALISM AND A NEW SOCIAL ORDER

ANSON G. PHELPS LECTURESHIP ON EARLY AMERICAN HISTORY

Volumes published by New York University Press:

D. Plooij, *The Pilgrim Fathers from a Dutch Point of View* (1932)

Andrew C. McLaughlin, *The Foundations of American Constitutionalism* (1932)

Charles M. Andrews, *Our Earliest Colonial Settlements: Their Diversities of Origin and Later Characteristics* (1933)

Samuel Eliot Morison, *The Puritan Pronaos: Studies in the Intellectual Life of New England in the Seventeenth Century* (1936)

Dixon Ryan Fox, *Yankees and Yorkers* (1940)

Evarts B. Greene, *Religion and the State: The Making and Testing of an American Tradition* (1941)

Leonard W. Labaree, *Conservatism in Early American History* (1948)

Thomas J. Wertenbaker, *The Golden Age of Colonial Culture* (1949)

Carl Bridenbaugh, *The Colonial Craftsman* (1950)

Wesley Frank Craven, *The Legend of the Founding Fathers* (1956)

Richard Harrison Shryock, *Medicine and Society in America: 1660–1860* (1960)

Edmund S. Morgan, *Visible Saints: The History of a Puritan Idea* (1963)

Louis Booker Wright, *The Dream of Prosperity in Colonial America* (1965)

Merrill Jensen, *The American Revolution Within America* (1974)

Brooke Hindle, *Emulation and Invention* (1981)

Joyce Appleby, *Capitalism and a New Social Order: The Republican Vision of the 1790s* (1983)

Capitalism and a New Social Order:

The Republican Vision of the 1790s

JOYCE APPLEBY

New York University Press
New York and London
1984

Library of Congress Cataloging in Publication Data

Appleby, Joyce Oldham.
  Capitalism and a new social order.

  (Anson G. Phelps lectureship on early American
history)
  Includes bibliographical references and index.
  1. Political science—United States—History—
18th century. 2. Democratic Party (U.S.)—History—
18th century. 3. United States—Politics and government
—1789–1815. I. Title. II. Series.
JA84.U5A75 1983   320.5'0973   83-13359
ISBN 0-8147-0581-2

Clothbound editions of New York University Press books
are Smyth-sewn and printed on permanent and durable
acid-free paper.

For Ann who gave so generously of herself.

Contents

Preface

THE INVITATION to give the 1982 Phelps lectures reached me when I had returned to an older preoccupation with American liberalism and offered me the opportunity to join my work on seventeenth-century English economic thought to a more recent investigation of the material underpinnings of Jeffersonian democracy. In both of these studies I had tried to uncover how the market economy influenced the way people thought about politics and the human potential for purposefully reordering social institutions. Capitalism in these studies has figured, therefore, less as a system for producing and distributing goods and more as an intellectual stimulus to men and women trying to come to terms with the forces for change in their world.

My intellectual debts to those with whom I disagree are large. Having studied Thomas Jefferson before the publication of the works that have depicted him as a nostalgic defender of country party values, I was resistant to this view, but the recovery of the role of classical republican thought in revolutionary America has made it possible to appreciate why the Jeffersonians construed the Federalists as a threat. Similarly, the older scholarly tradition that presented the Jeffersonians as a Southern-based party with lineal connections to the Antifederalists made clear that it took the radical propensities and Enlightenment enthusiasms of the political newcomers in the middle states to recast American politics in the 1790s.

Despite the persistent appeal of Jeffersonian idealism in the United States, the material and moral underpinnings for the vision of a free society of independent men prospering through an expansive commerce in farm commodities

proved short-lived. The second great awakening undermined the secular faith in a natural social order and the
growth of industry strengthened the tendency of capitalism
to divide workers and employers. Both developments com-
promised the Jeffersonians' commitment to equality of opportunity and esteem. By emphasizing the democratic faith
that the Jeffersonians infused into their version of a capi-
talistic society, I hope to make more salient the contradic-
tions that lie at the heart of the American self-image.

I owe special thanks to Patricia Bonomi and Carl Prince
whose hospitality made my New York visit a very special
treat. I learned much from the questions posed by members
of the audience at the four Phelps lectures. Gary Nash, Paul
Clemens, and Martha Avery gave my manuscript the kind
of close reading that helped me clarify my ideas. Mark
Kleinman was unfailing in his good-humored search for lost
citations. A grant from the UCLA Academic Senate supported my research for this study. To all of these friends
and colleagues I am deeply grateful.

CAPITALISM AND A NEW SOCIAL ORDER

An English Frame of Reference

IN LATE 1865 Henry Yates Thompson, a Cambridge University graduate and wealthy Englishman of progressive sympathies, offered to endow a lectureship at his alma mater on the subject of America. Having recently returned from a tour of the United States, Thompson was excited about the possibility of sharing his new-found knowledge. He sketched the details of his offer in an official proposal to the vice chancellor. The lecturer was to be nominated by the president of Harvard to spend a term at Cambridge University every other year, at which time he would deliver a dozen lectures to undergraduates on "the History, Literature and Institutions of the United States of America." The need for some instruction on the United States had already been stressed that year by the great liberal politician, Richard Cobden, who had been warning English audiences of the dangers arising from their total ignorance of America. Not an Oxford or Cambridge undergradutate, Cobden charged, could have pointed out Chicago on a map even though it was a city that indirectly fed a million Englishmen.[1]

The dons of Cambridge, however, shared neither Cobden's worries nor Thompson's enthusiasm, and they

1. Ged Martin, "The Cambridge Lectureship of 1866: A False Start in American Studies," *Journal of American Studies*, 7 (1973), 17–29.

mounted a vigorous and successful campaign to get the proposed lectureship rejected by the Academic Senate. They outlined their fears on printed flyers that can still be read at the Cambridge library. The lectures, they said, would be the occasion for infecting undergraduates with republican principles. That the students in the Cambridge Union voted overwhelming approval of the Thompson lectureship only proved how very badly they needed guidance. One flyer explained why the bad effects from exposure to information about America could not be contained. If the undergraduates were filled with a love for democracy, they could not help spreading it broadcast and by this means produce "discontent and dangerous ideas among persons less educated than themselves, over whom they would naturally exercise some considerable influence." Another employed what has become one of my favorite oxymorons when he announced that the lectureship would be an arrangement by which Cambridge should be favored with "a biennial flash of Transatlantic darkness."[2]

Confronted with the implacable opposition of the Cambridge traditionalists, the proponents of the lectureship allowed the issue of teaching modern history to be diverted into a debate on the merits of American culture. Why, they asked lamely, did the Cambridge curriculum include so much about the republican institutions of Greece and Rome if republican principles and darkness were synonymous terms? Another supporter insisted that the Harvard credentials of the lecturers would guarantee that the lectures be inoffensive. Cambridge University, he maintained, would be neither Americanized nor democratized because the lecturers would be drawn from that class in the United States which felt itself "increasingly in danger of being swamped by the lower elements of a vast democracy." This defense only led to the jibes at the better class of Americans for "meekly

2. The printed flysheets can be found in the manuscripts room of the University Library of Cambridge University under the heading, "American Lectureship, 1865–6." Quoted flysheet was that of E.H. Perowne, the leading opponent from Corpus Christi College.

submitting to ejectment from public life." For a time it looked as though the debate would grind to halt until it could be decided whether it was beyond all doubt that the Harvard faculty was entirely composed of gentlemen.[3]

The serious side of the controversy was restored by H.R. Bailey of St. John's who nicely summarized why the lectureship posed a threat to both Cambridge University and English society as a whole. "The principles, which, I suppose, American citizens avow of Liberty, Equality and Fraternity," he said, "are not our principles [and] they are directly subversive of those upon which our institutions, civil and religious are founded. Government, authority, faith, submission, reverence—these are indissolubly bound together, and any shock to one part of the system must be felt throughout the whole." When the day of the balloting arrived the opponents packed the Senate house with Cambridgeshire clergymen who enjoyed university voting privileges, and the measure went down to defeat, 110 to 82.[4] The conflict over the American lectureship was in some ways a miniature of the great debate going on as Parliament prepared to vote on the reform bill of 1867. Throughout the nation that inseparable unity of church and state, aristocracy and commoners, king and people that the dons had been defending was being challenged by those like Cobden, who believed in progress, free trade, democracy, and knowing how to find Chicago on a map.

The last time a group of politicians in the United States publicly defended the traditional concept of society invoked by the Cambridge dons was in the 1790s. The defeat of the Federalists at the end of that decade signalled the defeat of the concept as well. Never again would any group of Americans seriously seeking power in a national election champion hierarchial values or deferential political practices. Men might continue to espouse the rule of the rich, the well-born, and the able but they would have to do it privately at

3. *Ibid.,* flysheet from A. Long, King's College.
4. *Ibid.,* flysheet of H.R. Bailey, St. John's College. See also Martin, "The Cambridge Lectureship of 1866," 24–29.

their clubs, or like the Harvard faculty members described in the Cambridge debates, withdraw from public life in order to preserve their purity.

In this volume I shall look at the demise of the venerable political tradition which the Federalists defended or, to put it more positively, I shall examine the elements that went into the triumph of the first truly American political movement, that of the Jeffersonian Republicans who swept into power in 1800. The Jeffersonians coalesced around a set of ideas—radical notions about how society should be reorganized. These ideas were propagated less by a class of men—that is, persons tied together by common economic interests—than by a kind of man—men attracted by certain beliefs. Their common vision about the reform of politics and the liberation of the human spirit made a national democratic party possible in the 1790s because that vision alone had the power to hold together otherwise quite disparate individuals and groups. Ideas—not interests or old loyalties or institutional identities—supplied the unity needed for success. Ideas joined a group of established elite reformers to a network of political interlopers; ideas attached the voters of the middle states to those of the south, confounding all expectations about regional coalitions. A distinctly secular conception of politics drew together in one voting bloc rationalists, free thinkers, and ardent members of a variety of evangelical sects. All of these alignments were necessary for the Republican victory in 1800.

American political culture changed decisively in that election. Men who believed in democracy found a national voice where in the past their strength had been local. The idea of limiting government became firmly associated with egalitarian goals. Popular sovereignty was reinterpreted to justify active, intrusive participation from the body of voters. Ordinary citizens formed voluntary political clubs, and newspapers editors took it upon themselves to report congressional debates and to publish highly critical evaluations of public officials and presidential policies. Election campaigns lost their genteel rhetoric about disinterested service, and candidates appealed openly to voters with their position on specific issues.[5] These activities have so exactly characterized American politics ever since 1800 that historians have had some difficulty coming to terms with what was novel—even revolutionary—about them at the time. There is nothing so hard to discover in the past as that which has subsequently become familiar. Yet in the 1790s there was something frightening about the rambunctious politicking that gave birth to the Jeffersonian Republican party. The success of this broadly based opposition to the Federalists—one bent on reforming political practices—meant, moreover, that instead of a gradual modification of American institutions and values there was an explicit reworking of them.

Drawing upon the radical implications in the American Revolution, the Jeffersonians overpowered the conservative elements that had survived the Independence movement. Their triumph at the level of ideology was so enduring that no politician would again think of defending the old order of an elite leadership and passive citizenry. Indeed, when an opposition to the triumphant Jeffersonians finally did form in the 1830s, it grew from the Jeffersonian ranks and constituted a variant of those same American principles that had so scandalized the Cambridge dons. Despite the Jefferson-Jackson Day dinners that the Democratic party held in my youth, it would be hard, I think, to determine whether Jefferson's mantle fit Jackson or Clay better.[6]

The main reason the 1790s witnessed a decisive change in American political culture is that there was something fundamental to decide. We can detect this in the behavior of the Federalists. They exuded the confidence of men

5. See, for instance, the description of the 1794 congressional election in Philadelphia in Roland M. Baumann, "Philadelphia's Manufacturers and the Excise Taxes of 1794: The Forging of the Jeffersonian Coalition," *Pennsylvania Magazine of History and Biographhy,* 106 (1982), 3–39. As Gary Nash has detailed in "The Transformation of Urban Politics 1700–1765," *Journal of American History,* 60 (1973), 605–32, many of these practices were familiar to colonial cities, particularly in the middle colonies. What is new is the national scope and ideological justification for them. In this connection, the location of the federal capital in New York and Philadelphia is significant.

6. Merrill D. Peterson, *The Jefferson Image in the American Mind* (New York, 1960), pp. 21–22, 69–73, 103–05.

whose views reflected deeply ingrained ways of thinking about politics. When public discourse turned polemical their voices became shrill, but they never lost their posture of protecting known truths about civil society. They knew that it was their opponents who were treading unfamiliar paths and they appealed to history and common sense to prove them wild visionaries. The Jeffersonians for their part took on the task of uncovering the propositions about human nature and society that underlay the Federalists' goals. They deliberately set up venerable ideas as the targets for their shafts of rhetoric. Pushed to expose the assumptions in each other's positions, the Federalists and the Jeffersonians made brilliantly clear that the character of America's future was at issue. By 1800 two coherent but opposing conceptions of society had emerged to polarize the voters' sympathies. This ideological cohesion ran well ahead of any economic or social integration within the United States.

The basis for the political divisions in the early national period has only become apparent during the past two decades since research on the character and structure of colonial society has revealed how deeply conservative many colonial communities were and hence how much was at stake when accepted ways of thinking and acting were challenged after the Revolution. Not too long ago historians were quite sure that the English had traveled very lightly to the New World. In fact the authority, faith, submission, and reverence that the King's College don had described as indissolubly connected were among those things scholars thought the colonists had left at the dock when they set sail for America. It was so easy to imagine those intrepid men and women—the ones with enough get up and go to leave Europe—landing in the proverbial wilderness and setting to work immediately to clear the fields, build homes, and convert the natural abundance around them into vendible commodities, somehow knowing that they were working to bring forth a new nation with a government of the people, by the people, and for the people. Implicit in this description is a view of European culture—the one the colonists brought with them—as a set of arbitrary restraints that held in check men's natural ability to take care of themselves. Without the restrictions of old world institutions, it was suggested, latent human tendencies could manifest themselves and each individual's natural propensity to seek self-improvement would come to the fore.[7]

Colonial historians during the past twenty years have demonstrated that America was not born free, rich, and modern. By looking closely at the details of ordinary life, they have transformed our conception of the American past and made salient the strength of traditional mores among common people. The Bible Commonwealth that Perry Miller had described as a blueprint in the minds of Puritan magistrates, we now know, found its master builders in the plain Puritans who formed covenanted communities across eastern Massachusetts and western Connecticut. Far from turning into modern entrepreneurs, Puritan men became rural patriarchs in towns remarkable for their cohesion and stability. They commanded their wives, controlled their adult sons and daughters, and kept out any deviants who might spoil the sweet harmony of their peaceable kingdoms.[8]

In the South recent research has revealed a hierarchial society presided over by families far more interested in imitating the ways of the English gentry than in exercising independent American tastes. The men of these families modeled their behavior after England's local magnates. They owned their labor force, they monopolized the good land,

7. This was the dominant theme of historical writing in the 1950s as exemplified in Daniel Boorstin, *The Americans: The Colonial Experience* (New York, 1959); Louis Hartz, *The Liberal Tradition in American History* (New York, 1955); Robert E. Brown, *Middle Class Democracy in Massachusetts and the Revolution* (Ithaca, N.Y., 1955); and Carl N. Degler, *Out of Our Past: The Forces that Shaped Modern America* (New York, 1959).

8. This interpretation rests upon the scholarship found in Philip J. Greven, Jr., *Four Generations: Population, Land and Family in Colonial Andover, Massachusetts* (Ithaca, N.Y., 1970); Kenneth Lockridge, *A New England Town, The First Hundred Years: Dedham, Massachusetts, 1636–1736* (New York, 1970); Michael Zuckerman, *Peaceable Kingdoms: New England Towns in the Eighteenth Century* (New York, 1970); James A. Henretta, *The Evolution of American Society, 1700–1815: An Interdisciplinary Analysis* (Lexington, Ma., 1973); Richard Bushman, *From Puritan to Yankee: Character and the Social Order in Connecticut, 1690–1765* (Cambridge, Ma., 1967); David Grayson Allen, *In English Ways* (Chapel Hill, 1981); and Robert A. Gross, *The Minutemen and Their World* (New York, 1976).

they ran both local and provincial government, and they overawed their poorer neighbors. Proud, self-assertive, and impulsive, the reigning planters of the Chesapeake, we have learned from Rhys Isaac and Timothy Breen, reinforced their political rule through carefully staged performances at dancing assemblies, horse races, cock fights, and court sessions. Ordinary members of society were turned into supernumeraries in these public dramas of the elite. When the humble white folk of Southern society rebelled against this cultural domination, it was not by espousing the radical philosophy of John Locke, but rather by embracing the fellowship offered by Baptist congregations. Indeed, North and South, the religious revivals of mid–eighteenth-century America offered an outlet for the discontented, a means for common people to assert themselves collectively against the overbearing authority of their social superiors. But the message of the revivalists was atavistic: a summons to return to a purer form of devotion, to make a more profound commitment of one's life to God—above all to reject those telltale signs of creeping secularism—absorption with material well-being, and justifications for self-interest.[9]

In intellectual history too, recent scholarship has challenged the old notion that the colonists were either Lockean liberals or Enlightenment men. Instead we have been taught through the work of Bernard Bailyn and Gordon Wood that the ideas that animated colonial leaders were ancient ones, going back to classical texts of politics rendered accessible to eighteenth-century readers by the English Commonwealthmen or Country party writers. These classical views that we now see as shaping the colonial consciousness involved assumptions very much at odds with a progressive conception of history. Classical theory emphasized that civil society was fragile, that men lusted after power, that stabil-

9. Rhys Isaac, *The Transformation of Virginia, 1740–1790* (Chapel Hill, 1982); T.H. Breen, *Puritans and Adventurers: Change and Persistence in Early America* (New York, 1980), and idem, "Horses and Gentlemen: The Cultural Significance of Gambling Among the Gentry of Virginia," *William and Mary Quarterly*, 34 (1977), 239–57; Alan Heimert, *Religion and the American Mind* (Cambridge, Ma., 1966); and Gary B. Nash, *The Urban Crucible: Social Change, Political Consciousness, and the Origins of the American Revolution* (Cambridge, Ma., 1979).

ity required a carefully constructed constitution. It also taught that there were two orders of men—the talented few and the ordinary many—and because there were inevitable social divisions, a properly balanced constitution would balance the powers of these two groups. But constitutional stability rested ultimately in this classical paradigm upon the exercise of civic virtue—upon the capacity of some men to rise above private interests and devote themselves to the public good. Men deeply involved in their own business, in getting ahead, and seizing opportunities for gain were not proper candidates for public office. Commerce which prompted private interests therefore threatened civil order. Ideally property should not serve as a way of making money, but rather, as J.G.A. Pocock has said, as a means of anchoring the individual in the structure of power and virtue and liberating him to practice these activities. In this classical political tradition men realized their fullest potential in politics, in serving the public good, and protecting the constitution.[10]

What we have learned about the social structure and the exercise of authority in colonial America is congruent with the central propositions of classical republican thought. Compatible too was the concept of human nature in Protestant theology. Men and women were prone to sin, and civil order was hard to maintain. Liberty depended upon the solution to difficult political problems. The values associated with free enterprise and greater productivity—what we would call capitalism—did not inspire confidence, but rather provoked anxiety. Like so many elements of English thinking that found their way into the colonial consciousness, the concepts of balanced government and of political participation based upon secure property embodied the ideals of an upper class that had arrogated to itself the unique qualifications for assuming power. They also reflected the yearning for tranquility in an age newly intro-

10. Bernard Bailyn, *The Ideological Origins of the American Revolution* (Cambridge, Ma., 1967); Gordon Wood, *The Creation of the American Republic, 1776–1787* (Chapel Hill, 1969); and J.G.A. Pocock, *The Machiavellian Moment: Florentine Political Thought and the Atlantic Republican Tradition* (Princeton, 1975), pp. 389–91.

duced to the disruptive force of an expanding economy. Far from colonial society diverging steadily from English ways, what we actually find in eighteenth-century America is a pervasive Anglicization that can be traced to several mutually reinforcing developments.

After three—sometimes four—generations many colonial towns had acquired a settled look. Strong community ties had finally materialized in the networks of families that only time can create. The fathers' authority at home and in town meetings assured stability and continuity. Fathers often arranged marriages, controlled inheritance, and used both law and custom to subordinate individual desires to the goals of the group. The economic development promoted by the flourishing Atlantic trade had brought new concentrations of wealth to the older colonies. Translated into cultural terms this meant that moneyed families could build handsome town houses and country estates. They imported carriages, put their servants into livery, and reared their children for genteel living. Imitating European tastes, they created the visible signs for the theoretical distinction between the few and the many.[11]

Although material abundance was widely diffused in the colonies, commercial growth increased the number of landless and decreased the holdings of land of those in the bottom ranks. In part this was because a more complex economy called into being more tradesmen whose wealth was in tools and skills, but it also reflected the relentless dynamic of market growth to consolidate disadvantages as well as advantages. To lose one's access to property at a time of rising land prices is to alter fundamentally one's long-term pros-

11. Jack P. Greene, "The Social Origins of the American Revolution: An Evaluation and an Interpretation," *Political Science Quarterly*, 88 (1973); Kenneth A. Lockridge, "Social Change and the Meaning of the American Revolution," *Journal of Social History*, 4 (1973); and idem, "Land, Population, and the Evolution of New England Society," *Past and Present*, no. 39 (1968); James A. Henretta, "Economic Development and Social Structure in Colonial Boston," *William and Mary Quarterly*, 22 (1965); Gary B. Nash and James T. Lemon, "The Distribution of Wealth in Eighteenth-Century America: A Century of Change in Chester County, Pennsylvania, 1693–1802," *Journal of Social History*, 2 (1968); and Allan Kulikoff, "The Progress of Inequality in Revolutionary Boston," *William and Mary Quarterly*, 28 (1971).

pects. Historians have named this process one of European-
ization because the division between rich and poor, which
had been modified during the initial period of settlement,
reappeared. Ordinary colonists frequently expressed great
bitterness at the ostentatious displays of wealth and the first
evidence of real poverty in America. What was a traditional
class structure in the old world appeared as an ugly novelty
in the new. To be sure, in mid–eighteenth-century America
there was a large bulge in the center of the social pyramid
and still no apex of enormous wealth. People in the mid-
dling ranks predominated; those propertyless poor at the
bottom represented a minority of white men, distinguished
as often by age as any other factor. But the abrupt swings
in the trade cycles—the ups and down occasioned by an international market still in the making—led to uncertainty.
Americans even then depended upon credit. The very
promise of their wealth-producing capacity facilitated borrowing and exposed them to the temptations and punish-
ments of social mobility.[12]

The English government also promoted Anglicization.
Plans to send an Anglican bishop to America were bruited
about as were schemes to create a provincial nobility. The An-
glo-French wars tied the colonies closer to Great Britain and
made representatives of the crown more aware of colonial
conditions. The growing importance of colonial markets led
to an increase in the number of British officials posted to
America. With their wives and daughters serving as fashion
plates, His Majesty's governors, customs officials, and naval
officers brought to colonial society the refined tastes that
upper-class colonists yearned to acquire. To become an out-
post of English culture in the New World was to maintain a

12. Marc Egnal, "The Economic Development of the Thirteen Continental
Colonies, 1720 to 1775," *Ibid.,* 32 (1975); and G.B. Warden, "Inequality and Instability in Eighteenth-Century Boston: A Reappraisal," *Journal of Interdisciplinary
History,* 6 (1976). For an assessment of the relative importance of instability and
inequality in Boston, see William Pencak, "The Social Structure of Revolutionary
Boston: Evidence from the Great Fire of 1760," *Journal of Interdisciplinary History,*
10 (1979), 267–78. For the effects of market instabilities, especially those associated with the conversion from tobacco crops to grains, see Paul G.E. Clemens,
*From Tobacco to Grain: The Atlantic Economy and the Development of Maryland's Eastern
Shore to 1776* (Ithaca, 1981).

psychic as well as a material connection with Europe. As this connection grew stronger members of the colonial elite found it easier to interpret their world through the conceptual categories of English political thought.[13]

When the recent research on social and intellectual developments in colonial America is brought together there is a nice fit. In small communities the fathers of the towns ran things. At the provincial level power went to those distinguished by their family, their wealth, their education, and the genteel bearing that could exact deference from others. Not having inherited their position, these leaders talked in broad terms about rational men, merit and virtue, the common good. As men of property and standing, they could always call upon the invidious contrast between the talented few and the vulgar many. When compliant, ordinary men and women figured in their thinking as sober, humble, and possessed of common sense. When caught up in religous revivals or tumultuous gatherings they were seen as enthusiastical, giddy, unruly, passionate—in short, "the unthinking multitude."

During the course of the eighteenth century, upper-class colonists became more independent as well as more English. Warfare and commercial development brought them closer to the mother country, but their own population and economic growth made America more powerful. The classical republican ideas they had picked up from the English country party taught them to beware of political corruption and to fear designs upon their liberties. English efforts to reform the imperial system were easily interpreted as signs of a conspiracy. As John Murrin has pointed out, the colonial resistance movement that ended in revolution began as a typical old-regime quarrel between corporate bodies over the boundaries of their respective privileges and authority. It

13. Thomas Bradbury Chandler, *An Appeal to the Public in Behalf of the Church of England in America* (New York, 1767); Edmund S. Morgan and Helen M. Morgan, *The Stamp Act Crisis: Prologue to Revolution* (Chapel Hill, 1953), p. 30; John M. Murrin, "The Great Inversion, or Court versus Country: A Comparison of the Revolution Settlements in England (1688–1721) and America (1776–1816)," in J.G.A. Pocock, ed., *Three British Revolutions: 1641, 1688, 1776* (Princeton, 1980); and Bailyn, *The Ideological Origins of the American Revolution.*

turned into a rebellion when the American elite failed to control the ordinary colonists who had lept into the fray with grievances of their own. The unexpected vigor and independence of these men acted as a constant pressure to widen and intensify the conflict. In this development we see a major structural difference between England and the colonies, one that was to be as important in the 1790s as in the 1760s. There existed in America no large, menacing body of dispossessed men to remind the propertied classes of their need to stick together. The very stability and well-being of the great majority of colonists permitted resistance to turn into rebellion and rebellion to revolution. Without the fear of a social upheaval, the elite itself splintered, Loyalists breaking off from Whigs as Antifederalists later would from Federalists and Jeffersonians from supporters of the Washington administration.[14]

Still, despite this fissiparous action, established leaders of New England and Virginia charted the course of revolutionary action and continued to exercise a disproportionate influence in the new state governments. In New York, Pennsylvania and New Jersey, where the established leaders failed to carry their people into rebellion, new men arose to supply the deficiency in leadership. After the war, these politicians frequently spoke out for popular reforms in voting, taxation, and land sales. When challenged by new men and measures the old elite—particularly in Massachusetts, New York, Pennsylvania, and New Jersey—threw its support behind a constitutional convention that would create an entirely new center of national power, one it could expect to control.[15] Both the first elections under the U.S.

14. Murrin, "The Myths of Colonial Democracy and Royal Decline in Eighteenth-Century America," *Cithara*, 5 (1965); and Dietmar Rothermund, *The Layman's Progress: Religion and Political Experience in Colonial Pennsylvania, 1740–1770* (Philadelphia, 1961), pp. 140–43. In Rothermund's words: "These leaders could not divide and rule the masses; instead they were divided and ruled by the masses themselves. Consequently no coherent elite with a group solidarity of its own could develop."

15. Edward Countryman, *A People in Revolution: The American Revolution and Political Society in New York, 1760–90* (Baltimore, 1981); Richard Alan Ryerson, *The Revolution is Now Begun: The Radical Committees of Philadelphia, 1765–1776* (Philadelphia, 1978); Thomas L. Purvis, "High-Born, Long-Recorded Families: Social

Constitution and the bold fiscal program of Washington's Secretary of the Treasury, Alexander Hamilton, signalled that a new national elite was in the process of solidifying its position in the politics, the economy, and the society of the new American nation. Indeed, without the eruption of a tumultuous popular movement in the 1790s the course of American politics might have mirrored that of England's where an economically progressive propertied class kept radical reform at bay for another century.

With this new understanding of the colonial era, it is easy to accept the Federalists' presumption that they and not their opponents were speaking for a conception of civil order deeply rooted in American values. What now needs to be explored are the origins of those Jeffersonian values that appear to us so quintessentially American. Like the classical version espoused by the Federalists, Jeffersonian republicanism began in an English frame of reference, though as the reaction of the Cambridge dons shows, the English upper class had repudiated it. Voltaire once described history as a pack of tricks that the present plays on the past. He failed to mention that the people of the past have their own dissembling pranks. The most troublesome for historians is the tendency to change without notice the meaning of words. Whole new concepts can take shape behind an unvarying set of terms. Virtue is such a one. In the context of classical republican thought virtue meant civic virtue, the quality that enabled men to rise above private interests in order to act for the good of the whole. By the 1780s this meaning is less clear. Speakers begin to add a modifier to make their point, as when John Adams said that "disinterested virtue is disappearing among us." When

Origins of New Jersey Assemblymen, 1703 to 1776," *William and Mary Quarterly*, 37 (1980), 613–15; Van Beck Hall, *Politics Without Parties: Massachusetts, 1780–1791* (Pittsburgh, 1972); Robert A. Becker, *Revolution, Reform and the Politics of American Taxation, 1763–1783* (Baton Rouge, 1980); and Jon C. Teaford, *The Municipal Revolution in America: Origins of Modern Urban Government, 1650–1825* (Chicago, 1975). As James Henderson pointed out in "The Structure of Politics in the Continental Congress," Stephen G. Kurtz and James H. Hutson, eds., *Essays on the American Revolution* (Chapel Hill, 1973), pp. 183–84, Virginians actually took the lead in calling for a constitutional convention for reasons that had more to do with national expansion than elitist anxieties.

Theodore Sedgwick wrote Rufus King, "the aristocracy of virtue is destroyed; personal influence at an end," he was using the word in the classical republican sense, but by the end of the century virtue more often referred to a private quality, a man's capacity to look out for himself and his dependents—almost the opposite of classical virtue.[16]

Historians are much better off when new words, such as individual, come into use. At the beginning of the seventeenth century individual was first applied to human beings to denote a single person, as opposed to society or the family, and not until Tocqueville's *Democracy in America* do we get the word individualism.[17] The increased use of the word individual in the eighteenth century entitles us to suspect at least that men appeared more and more as separate, autonomous entities than as members of some collectivity, just as the occasional reference to women in public discourse strongly suggests their absence from the mind of those countless writers who speak only of men. Thomas Paine gave currency to the word, equality, while liberty and popular sovereignty underwent transformations at the end of the eighteenth century. More important, the social theories that defined them changed.[18] No other political ideal was invoked more often in the Anglo-American world than that of liberty, yet its meaning was far from precise. No, that is incorrect. Its meaning was precise in particular intellectual contexts, of which there were at least three which speakers might have in mind in the seventeenth and eighteenth centuries. But only scholars talk about things like

16. As cited in Thomas Lawrence Davis, "Aristocrats and Jacobins in Country Towns: Party Formation in Berkshire County, Massachusetts (1775–1816)" (Boston University dissertation, 1975), p. 321. As Davis noted, vi., Federalists continually called for an "aristocracy of virtue."

17. *The Compact Edition of the Oxford English Dictionary* (Oxford, 1971), I, 1419, lists the sense, "A single human being, as opposed to Society, the Family, etc." first in 1626, "Individualism" appearing in the Reeve 1840 translation of De Tocqueville's *Democracy in America*, III, 203.

18. Thomas Paine's *Common Sense* is noteworthy for having demeaned the classical republican concept of liberty while exalting equality as a political goal. In this connection it is interesting to note that the Cambridge don quoted on p. 3 ascribed to Americans a faith in the French Revolutionary ideals of "Liberty, Equality and Fraternity" rather than the "Life, Liberty, and the Pursuit of Happiness" affirmed in the Declaration of Independence.

"intellectual contexts." In everyday life we use words as though their meaning were stable and widely shared. A good deal of the passion of the political debates of the 1790s can be attributed to the anger and confusion the disputants felt at the differing ways central concepts like sovereignty, equality, and liberty were being used.

Probably the least familiar concept of liberty used then was that most common to us—that is, liberty as personal freedom bounded only by such limits as are necessary if others are to enjoy the same extensive personal freedom. Before the Revolution liberty more often referred to a corporate body's right of self-determination. Within countless communities the ambit of freedom might well be circumscribed, yet men would speak of sacrificing their lives for liberty—the liberty of the group to have local control. In the classical republican tradition discussed earlier—that ornate theory about the constitutional balance between the one, the few, and the many—liberty was a cherished goal and its essence was political. To be a free man (and they always were men) was to participate in the life of the polis or community. To have liberty was to share in the power of the state, to be actively involved in making and executing decisions. Thus liberty in this sense was associated with a republic—the rule of law—and could not exist in a monarchy where the will of the king or queen was supreme. Liberty in the classical republican tradition pertained to the public realm and not the private. Indeed, it was the capacity of men to rise above personal interest that made republics and therefore liberty possible. Virtue and liberty were indissolubly linked in classical republican theory. From the time of the Glorious Revolution, Englishmen in the ruling class could feel themselves in possession of this classical liberty because their mixed, constitutional monarchy had created a new sovereign, that of the King in Parliament. Colonists considering their own legislatures to be copies of the British Parliament responded equally warmly to the ancient ideal of free men realizing their human potential in service to the commonwealth.[19]

19. Pocock, *Machiavellian Moment,* pp. 401–552; see also Jack P. Greene, "Political Mimesis: A Consideration of the Historical and Cultural Roots of Legislative

The classical republican definition of liberty appealed especially to men whose talents and superior position in society encouraged them to identify strongly with the group as a whole. For this reason the liberty of classical republicanism bears careful examination. For instance, the assertion that society is divided between the few and the many—the elite and the common people—is an assertion of human inequality presumed to be rooted in nature and therefore unavoidable in social practice. It is because of this inequality that the few, defined either as an hereditary nobility or those who held property, were given a separate house in the legislature. The disproportionate amount of power given to the few was in turn justified, because without their check upon popular power liberty itself would be lost to everyone as one or the other group gained ascendency and ruled in its own interest. Writers in the classical republican tradition—James Harrington, John Trenchard, and Thomas Gordon—illustrated these principles with references to the civil wars, tyrannies, and usurpations so replete in the histories of Greece and Rome. Although classical republicanism offered the possibility of establishing an enduring republic where men might enjoy the liberty of civic participation, the theory itself was grounded in an historical realism that cautioned against having too high hopes, given the fickle, power-lusting nature of men.

Equally rooted in history was another concept of liberty familiar to Englishmen on both sides of the Atlantic. This was the liberty of secure possession—the enjoyment of legal title to a piece of property or the privilege of doing a particular thing without fear of arrest or punishment. Unlike classical republican liberty, this kind of liberty was negative, private, and limited. When people talked about these liberties, they referred to promises between the ruler and the ruled that carried no implications about the kind of rule that prevailed. Preserved in custom and the common law,

Behavior in the British Colonies in the Eighteenth Century," *American Historical Review,* 75 (1969); Bernard Bailyn, "A Comment," *ibid.;* Greene, "Reply," *Ibid.;* and Paul Lucas, "A Note on the Comparative Study of the Structure of Politics in Mid–Eighteenth-Century Britain and its American Colonies," *William and Mary Quarterly,* 28 (1971).

specified by documents, interpreted through formal procedures, such promises formed the ligaments of the body politic. While law courts were developed to implement these promises, the liberty of secure possession could be enjoyed under a monarchy or aristocracy or in a democracy. Nor need the liberties be spread throughout the populace. The ancient distinctions between freemen and denizens or freemen and villeins reminds us of this. These liberties did not flow from a theory of government, but rather from specific arrangements that in time became institutionalized. They were concrete and verifiable.[20] When colonists in the 1760s spoke of the rights and privileges of Englishmen, they had in mind this meaning of liberty. Their outrage at the stamp tax, the Quartering Act, and the various reforms of the American customs fed on the sense of betrayal implicit in a broken promise. In the ensuing debates about the status of the charters and precedents which the colonists thought guaranteed their liberties, this outrage turned to despair, for they heard Parliament make claim to a sovereign authority totally incompatible with their concept of liberty.

Liberty in the classical republican paradigm and liberty in the historic rights tradition are distinct and potentially contradictory concepts. The classical liberty of freemen to participate in political decisions celebrates the public arena and the disinterestedness of civic virtue. The liberty of secure possession protects private, personal enjoyments—liberties that become vested interests. There is no suggestion of limiting the power of government in the classical tradition as long as that power serves the common good, whereas the particular liberties of citizens or subjects secured by law limits the scope of public authority. Classical republican liberty is a lofty ideal; the liberty of legal rights pertains to the mundane and everyday aspects of living. Despite these dissimilarities, these two meanings could and did merge with one another, particularly in those moments when men feared the loss of their liberty, however defined. The classical republican theory was after all a particular solution to the en-

20. This concept of liberty is most trenchantly explored in Jack Hexter's review of *The Machiavellian Moment* in *History and Theory*, 16 (1977).

during political predicament: how to secure liberty when its enjoyment required order and order was most efficiently achieved through the imposition of the ruler's will. History was a record of usurpations as kings, nobles, and popular assemblies vaulted over the limits of law. Monarchies became tyrannies, aristocracies oligarchies, while democracies dissolved into chaos as ruling groups forsook the good of the whole. Subject to attack from without and corruption from within, civil society indeed seemed imperilled, and the source of the peril was human nature itself. England's mixed constitution, with its balance of monarchical, aristocratic, and democratic elements, held out hope, but wise men read their histories and kept a careful watch.

A third meaning of liberty one could encounter in the public discourses in the Anglo-American world of the eighteenth century entered the political lexicon in the mid-seventeenth century. Often called Lockean in reference to the great political philosopher, John Locke, its distinctive characteristics actually came from Thomas Hobbes, and I shall talk about it as the liberal concept of liberty. It is a tribute to the scholarly virtuosity of Bernard Bailyn and J.G.A. Pocock that we no longer believe, as generations of historians before us have, that America's revolutionary leaders were simple Lockean liberals, though it would be a mistake to underestimate the early influence of the social contract theorists.[21] Unlike the classical and legal meanings of liberty, the liberal conception ignores history as a source of guidance. Hobbes and Locke and the succession of writers who followed them reasoned from an imaginary account of man in the state of nature to an abstract definition of liberty. More analytical than didactic, the liberal theory rationalized government by deriving its function from general proposi-

21. Locke's relative unimportance was initially suggested by John Dunn in "The Politics of Locke in England and America in the Eighteenth Century," in John W. Yolton, ed., *John Locke: Problems and Perspectives* (Cambridge, 1969). For more recent assessments of Locke's influence see Lois G. Schwoerer, *The Declaration of Rights, 1689* (Baltimore, 1982); Morton White, *The Philosophy of the American Revolution* (Oxford, 1978), pp. 20–29, 221–54; Merrill D. Peterson, *Thomas Jefferson and the New Nation* (New York, 1979), pp. 64–65; and Isaac Kramnick, "Republican Revisionism Revisited," *American Historical Review*, 87 (1982), pp. 629–64.

tions about human nature and the formation of civil society. Twentieth-century readers are struck by Hobbes's description in the *Leviathan* of life in the state of nature as "solitary, poor, nasty, brutish and short." But Hobbes's contemporaries in mid–seventeenth-century England found little startling in this. After all, they heard about the fallen state of man in much more graphic terms almost every Sunday. Neither poets nor dramatists—certainly not historians—offered a prettier picture of human nature. What shocked contemporaries about Hobbes was his insistence that men were naturally equal. "Methinks," wrote one of Hobbes's most vehement critics, "that he discourses of Men as if they were terrigene, born out of the earth, come up like Seeds, without any relation one to the other." By nature, the critic continued, man was "made a poor helples Child who confides and trusts in his Parents, and submits to them."[22]

It was men's equal ability to achieve their own ends that created the brutish state of nature, according to Hobbes, and explained why men consented to put themselves under the rule of an absolute sovereign who could produce order so that they might enjoy peace and commodious living. Writing a generation after Hobbes, Locke accepted his method of starting with an abstract model of the state of nature—or the absence of civil society—in order to determine what civil society contributed. Unlike Hobbes, Locke gave all men a conscience and a specific injunction—the law of nature—which taught them that since all mankind are "equal and independent, no one ought to harm another in his life, health, liberty or possessions." With these premises Locke put together his famous explanation for the origin of government. Living free and equal in a state of nature with the protection of natural law, men formed civil society only for convenience. By giving up their private right to execute the law of nature they created government to do the policing, but civil society added nothing to their rights nor to the content of natural law; it existed only to implement what was already a part of God's creation. Its power, most impor-

22. William Lucy, *Observations, Censures and Confutation of Notorious Errours in Mr. Hobbes His Leviathan* (London, 1663).

tantly, was limited to those measures necessary to protect the life, liberty, and property of the members of society. So fundamental were they to civil society that revolution itself was justified when it became abundantly clear that a particular government no longer served those ends.[23]

To recapitulate the argument alone fails to do justice to the effect of Hobbes's and Locke's reasoning, for to follow their logic in the seventeenth century was to be liberated from the awe and reverence—at a minimum the didacticism—that accompanied discussions of sovereign authority. Nothing turned out to be more subversive than the analytical spirit that the liberal approach encouraged. Instrumental, utilitarian, individualistic, egalitarian, abstract, and rational, the liberal concept of liberty was everything that the classical republican concept was not. So at odds were these two liberties that it is hard to understand how they could have coexisted in the same political discourse. That is a puzzle yet to be solved. A clue to it lies in the use put to the various theories. Locke offered a rationale and a justification for bringing an autocratic ruler to heel. His theories took shape and circulated when England's Parliamentary leaders sought to displace James II in the 1680s. Classical republicanism flourished during those periods when the English upper class either anticipated or enjoyed political power. Its civic humanism offered a concept of public life that served the moral and intellectual needs of the ruling English gentry. By emphasizing the organic nature of human society, classical republicanism gave the talented few a critical function as the brains of the body politic, just as the Lockean appeal to individual rights encouraged the exertions of all in a revolutionary situation. Well known to the colonists, Locke's lucid explanation of the origins of government was pushed to the fore during the crisis over Parliamentary taxation in the 1760s.

Initially the colonists had insisted that they were protecting the rights of Englishmen. Only when it became clear

23. Thomas Hobbes, *The Leviathan* (London, 1651), chapter 18; and John Locke, *Second Treatise of Government* (London, 1689), sections 4–14, 123–42, 202–204.

that their interpretation of the imperial crisis was not shared in the mother country did colonial rebels shift ground from the historic rights of English subjects to the abstract rights of all men. Then, as with an earlier high-minded group of English leaders, Locke's right to revolution offered a justification for opposing one's sovereign, a heinous crime in a world still knit together by loyalty. After the Revolution, both Lockean liberal and classical republican liberty figured in American political discourse. We might say that the several meanings of liberty were like elements suspended in a solution, awaiting the catalyst that would crystalize them. It was not long in coming for the gentlemen constitution-drafters who had spent the summer of 1787 together in Philadelphia. In the very months that many of them were settling into their new offices under that constitution in New York, the catalytic agent appeared in the form of the French Revolution. In the ensuing decade the full implications of the liberal concept of liberty were clarified and its fundamental incompatibility with the venerable classical tradition made starkly apparent.

It is the modern notion of liberty that undergirds the free enterprise system which received its political framework in America with the adoption of the constitution. This liberal definition of liberty, I will argue, also gave shape and direction to "the Republican Vision of the 1790s" which forms the subject of this volume. The capitalism in my title of course refers to a way of organizing the economy—a particular system for producing and distributing the material goods that sustain and embellish life. The word has acquired as well the protean characteristics of an ideal, a symbol, a myth and a shibboleth which also figure in its history. In the eighteenth century two features of the market economy fascinated contemporaries: the reliance upon individual initiative and the absence of authoritarian direction. Increasingly private arrangements were counted upon to supply the public's material needs. At the same time the productive goal of making wealth to produce wealth supplanted the older notion of wealth as the maintainer of status. In these transformations we come close to the conceptual heart of capitalism, for money becomes capital through the changed intentions of those with the money, that is, with the decision to invest rather than spend or hoard wealth. We need to keep in mind the novelty of all these elements when we assess how men and women in the 1790s responded to the elaboration of the market economy.

The "new social order and Republican vision" in my title points to a change in thinking about human association in the late eighteenth century. A hundred years earlier, as we have seen, people spoke of the state of nature, a predicament, and civil society, a solution. A century and a quarter of economic development had dramatically enhanced public opinon about voluntary human actions, and society was the word that emerged to represent the uncoerced relations of people living under the same authority. "Society," Paine wrote in *Common Sense,* "is produced by our wants and government by our wickedness; the former promotes our happiness positively by uniting our affections, the latter negatively by restraining our vices."[24] It is this vision which animated the Jeffersonians and draws our attention to the role of ideas in their history, particularly those ideas that formed their imaginative construction of reality. By looking at the dramatic events of the 1790s in the United States, I hope also to say something in general about how economic activities, social movements, political institutions, and the ways men and women think about them impinge on each other. The particular ideas the Republicans and Federalists thought and fought with came from an English frame of reference, but it was only a frame of reference. They gave the ideas their operative meaning, working within their own situation in the polemics of the early national period. In the case of the Republicans the participants produced what Jefferson called Americanism, a political brew so heady that Cambridge undergraduates were not allowed to drink it until our century.

24. Philip S. Foner, ed., *The Complete Writings of Thomas Paine* (New York, 1945), I, 4.

The Promise
in Prosperity

WHEN EDMUND BURKE read Adam Smith's *Theory of Moral Sentiments* he was stirred by the genius it revealed. "A theory like yours founded on the nature of man, which is always the same," he wrote, "will last, when those that are founded on his opinions, which are always changing, will and must be forgotten." That Burke, who was sensitive to the elusive influences of beauty, poetry, and custom, should believe in a uniform human nature only underscores how completely the idea had triumphed in the second half of the eighteenth century. By 1776 Adam Smith had filled in the details of this nature of man in those memorable, quotable lines that are sprinkled through *The Wealth of Nations*. There Smith attributed the principle which prompts people to save to the desire of "bettering our condition, a desire which, though generally calm and dispassionate, comes with us from the womb, and never leaves us till we go into the grave." "In the whole interval which separates those two moments," he went on to explain, "there is scarce perhaps a single instant in which any man is so perfectly and completely satisfied with his situation, as to be without any wish of alteration or improvement of any kind."[1] In this exemplary passage Smith

1. As quoted in R.D. Collinson Black, "Smith's Contribution in Historical Perspective," in T. Wilson and A.S. Skinner, eds., *The Market and the State: Essays in Honour of Adam Smith* (Oxford, 1976); and Adam Smith, *An Inquiry into the Nature and Causes of the Wealth of Nations* (New York, 1937), pp. 324–25.

captured and universalized that ceaseless striving that has characterized Western men and women since the early modern period.

In this and similar statements we find not only a new conception of human motivation but the assertion that this behavior is true for all times and places. It was not a conditioned response to certain social forces, but rather a basic endowment that every human being brought into the world. Philosophers since Aristotle's time at least had talked about uniform qualities in human nature—though the term human nature belongs to the eighteenth century. What was new in Smith's writing and what made his contemporaries believe they had made discoveries previously undetected was the predictability of human behavior. Instead of the Greeks' essences and humors or the Christians' belief in the proneness to sin, eighteenth-century men spoke about the unvarying principles of human action.

A new field of investigation had in fact led to these observations about the consistent motivation of men and women. The phenomenal growth in human productivity had prompted dozens of English writers to examine economic relations as parts of an isolated system and in these writings a new definition of human nature had taken shape. Coming at the end of more than a century of investigation, Smith joined the drive for self-improvement to a mechanical principle—the division of labor—to demonstrate how nations grow wealthy. When the division of labor has been once thoroughly established, he explained, men supply by far the greater part of their wants by exchanging the surplus of their labor with that of other men's labor. "Every man," he said, "thus lives by exchanging, or becomes in some measure a merchant, and the society itself grows to be what is properly a commercial society."[2] In Smith's terms Great Britain had been a commercial society for less than a century. The American colonies had become one even more recently. What Smith did not realize was that his manner of reasoning about human nature was itself a product of a

2. *Ibid.*, p. 22.

commercial society and could be traced back to the first English publications on trade, which began appearing in the early seventeenth century.

In talking about the "promise in prosperity" I want to emphasize at the outset the negative, for the very possibility of material abundance had a profoundly unsettling effect, in as much as traditional political ideas were firmly rooted in the realities of a limited economic output. With ninety percent of the people's labor required to produce the food for the entire commonwealth and each of those life-supporting harvests subject to drastic reductions from bad weather or infestations, the survival of the whole was clearly linked to the diligence of each member. Well might the Puritan divine, Thomas Hooker, score individualism: "For if each man may do what is good in his owne eyes, proceed according to his own pleasure, so that none may crosse him or controll him by any power; there must of necessity follow the distraction and desolation of the whole." [3]

We can think of the struggle for daily subsistence as a protracted emergency. In a world in which famine could decimate the population, the preponderant part of the people lived familiarly with death. With so many lives always at risk, concern for the public good predominated. The precariousness of existence justified authoritarian control of economic life—the Tudor laws against forestalling, regrating, and engrossing come to mind—as well as the government's protection of the weak. The communities of the premodern world were knit together by necessity. To belong to a group meant to be under a social umbrella (we might consider the different imagery of the security net we hear so much about these days). Membership—a sense of place—was all-important to the single person and carried in its train the obligations and privileges of belonging.

The structural underpinnings for this traditional world view changed during the course of the sixteenth and seventeenth centuries. For over a hundred years, population growth, inflation, agricultural innovations, new forms of

3. Thomas Hooker, *A Survey of the Summe of Church-Discipline* (London, 1648), p. 188.

business association, and the intensification of European and world trade had worked cumulatively and interactively to transform the economy. The most important changes, particularly for England, were domestic, those associated with the elaboration of a single, national market. A new commercial network had been laid over the English countryside, bringing all but the most isolated areas into a unified economy. The glamorous foreign trades were integrated into the bread and butter commerce of everyday life. Rural shopkeepers began stocking the luxuries that the rich once went to London to purchase. Most important to the reconceptualization of human behavior, many of the new trade linkages were made by quite ordinary men—not the great merchants or landed magnates but cattle drovers and cheesemongers, peddlers and teamsters. These small fry created what economists call a commercial infrastructure. Because of the exigent distractions of civil unrest in the seventeenth century, the old system of economic regulation associated with the Tudors quite simply broke down. A broadside from the guild of household tradesmen published in 1675 epitomized the new situation. In it, the guild members complained bitterly that hawkers, contrary to the law, sold great quantities of goods in cities, towns, villages, and hamlets all over the kingdom. Formerly they would have been prosecuted, the broadside said, but now they prospered and had multiplied to at least 15,000 in number.[4] These same interlopers in old and new trades carried the productive ideal down the social ladder and out into the countryside.

During the second half of the seventeenth century England made a momentous breakthrough in its agriculture. The cumulative advantages of farming improvements led to such abundant harvests that England began exporting foodstuffs. After 1688 grain exporters got handsome bounties from the government. Thus the financial well-being of the

4. *Reasons humbly offered . . . by the Drapers, Mersers . . . and other trading housekeepers,* 1675. See also J.P. Cooper, "Economic Regulation and the Cloth Industry in Seventeenth-Century England," Royal Historical Society *Transactions,* 5th ser., 20 (1970); and Joyce Oldham Appleby, *Economic Thought and Ideology in Seventeenth-Century England* (Princeton, 1978), pp. 99–128.

landed gentry and nobility became as involved in foregin
trade as that of merchants. England had truly become that
commercial society Smith later talked about. Lower grain
prices in turn freed money for the purchases of spices, Indian calicoes, the new pottery, and materials for building in
the city and the country. More and more English men and
women could afford to indulge an exotic taste for sugar,
coffee, tea, and tobacco. Freedom from the fear of dearth—
a truly historic benchmark—explains in part the lapsing of
the ornate economic regulations of early modern England,
for it was the endemic fear of famine and food riots that
had goaded magistrates into enforcing those regulatory
statutes. Although no one challenged the right, indeed the
obligation, of royal authority to control economic activities
for the good of the whole, abundance encouraged a measure of relaxation. In fact, throughout the eighteenth century the ambit of economic freedom widened inside Great
Britain even as Parliament attempted to tighten its hold on
the trade of England's American colonies.[5]

Especially critical for the popularization of that view of
human nature that Edmund Burke hailed in Adam Smith's
writing was an utterly new phenomenon in seventeenth-
century England—an outpouring of publications on economic topics. Written by private men, not public officials,
often anonymously, and always claiming practical experience with the subject at hand, these pamphlets, treatises,
handbills, and broadsides introduced a number of ideas that
are noteworthy. First, the men who took up their pens to
write about coin shortages, interest rates, trade balances, and
agricultural improvements were aware that they were dealing with a novel force intruding upon a settled way of doing
things. They sometimes attacked these novelties, sometimes
justified them, but always explained them, and that meant
they were analyzing the mundane, prosaic activities they saw
around them. Cataloguing the influences at play in the

---

5. C.R. Fay, "The Miller and the Baker: A Note on Commercial Transition,
1770–1837," *Cambridge Historical Journal,* 1 (1923); and Walter J. Shelton, *English
Hunger and Industrial Disorders: A Study of Social Conflict during the First Decade of
George III's Reign* (Toronto, 1973).

ebullient English economy, certain authors discovered a pattern. They began to discern connections everywhere— effects of interest rates on agricultural investments, of wage rates upon foreign sales, of coin shortage on the volume of trade. The consequences of one action became the causes of another. Effects and causes produced conditions; conditions became variables open to manipulation. Through these rather ephemeral publications a concept of the market emerged as the market itself was taking shape. The word market was transformed, another of those sleights of tongues obscuring a change of meaning. Less and less did market refer to that palpable affair of village stalls and rustic hawkers, of wagons and carts lumbering toward a country town laden with the farmer's produce. Instead, market denoted an invisible flow of goods and payments girdling the globe and crisscrossing the English countryside. No one could see more than a tiny fraction of this market, so it began to figure as an abstraction, something that represented the aggregation of all market bargains condensed into a price, a number, a word that went back along the lines of communication to influence people's decision. "Let me sell as the market goes," readers were told, was the husbandman's creed. Another pamphleteer claimed that the market was the best judge of values.[6]

The actual round of economic activities in early modern England was not at all suggestive of uniformities. Raising and marketing food and fibers involved a thousand variations of soil, seed, technique, and lore. Weather changed from year to year. Bargains were influenced by the wits, information, resources, and moral latitude of those involved. To reduce these various influences at play in daily life to a system of generalizations represented an intellectual act of great consequences. Despite its evident diversity, the newly extended commercial system nonetheless suggested order to those who observed and analyzed it. Writers traced that order more and more to the human bargainers

6. John Cook, *Unum Necessarium* (London, 1648), p. 8; [Nicholas Barbon], *An Apology for the Builder* (London, 1685), pp. 32–33.

who put the flow of goods and payments in motion. Because more and more individuals exercised control over their resources with scant reference to old usages or even existing statutes, commercial writers treated these market participants as autonomous negotiators. Yet even though acting voluntarily, men and women seemed to converge on the same estimation of value. Behind this convergence analysts discerned the influence of the profit motive. Self-interested individuals determined value in their bargains; the aggregate of those discrete private bargains determined the rates and prices that prevailed over the entire market. Thus observers concluded that the law-like regularity of economic relations came from a consistent force inside each market participant.

Obvious—even banal—as these conclusions may appear to us, in seventeenth- and eighteenth-century England they had radical implications, for they meant that however socially differentiated people might be, in their market dealings there was an overriding similarity. Rich and poor, old and young, wise and innocent, male and female, genteel and vulgar, as buyers and sellers people revealed a common human nature. "All men by Nature are alike," Sir Josiah Child, the great merchant prince of the East India Company, once wrote, adding by way of emphasis, "as I have before demonstrated and Mr. Hobbs hath truly asserted." To give specificity to his point he amplified: "Shopkeepers like all other Men are led by their profit."[7] We find it a bit stale, and, I think, a little depressing to be told that people inevitably pursue personal advantage, but we are living at the end of this world view, not at the dawn when it contained exciting possibilities. Its social impact must be measured against the old conviction that human beings were impulsive, fickle, passionate, unruly, and likely to come to no good end regardless of what they did. Self-interest in market transactions presumed a rationality that was actually complimentary to human nature. Men and women made choices that

7. Sir Josiah Child, *A Discourse About Trade* (London, 1690), p. 125; idem, *A New Discourse of Trade* (London, 1693), p. 86.

served them well. When this self-interest was extended to the planting of the most profitable crops, the location of the best markets, borrowing at the cheapest rate, and calculating the optimal times to sell, a wide range of powers had been added to society through a new conception of human nature. Moralists lamented the materialism and here-now-ness of commercial preoccupations, but the economic writers who detailed the orderly round of buying and selling displayed an enthusiasm for these newly discovered attributes of ordinary people. They also often adopted that superior tone common when one is in the van of an intellectual movement and understands developments that are obscure to others.

Self-interest could only be accounted socially benign if it could be demonstrated that all this incessant striving after private ends did not lead to chaos. Herein of course lay the brilliance of Adam Smith's liberal economic theory, that marvelously detailed description of the way in which the urge to improve oneself through profitable exchanges prompted each to commit her and his resources most advantageously and, when disciplined by competition, led inexorably to the greatest good for society. No writer before Smith had had the wit to detail the workings of the invisible hand of the market, but the principle was clearly stated during the century before *The Wealth of Nations* was published in 1776. For example, an English landlord writing to defend the conversion of common fields into private farms had earlier claimed that whenever there was the least need for grain men would plant it for their own profit because "every one by the light of nature and reason will do that which makes for his greatest advantage." This seventeenth-century writer went on to make the crucial connection by adding that the advancement of private persons will be "the advantage of the publick." A generation later such observations had become commonplace as when Charles Davenant declaimed that "Trade is in its Nature free, finds its own Channel and best directs its own Course." Davenant's additional comment that "Wisdom is most commonly in the

Wrong, when it pretends to direct Nature" drew attention to the most protean implication of this new line of reasoning—the idea that market relations represented a natural system.[8]

It takes an act of imagination on our part to realize how startling it was to claim that the multifarious bargaining of commerce made up a natural system. As I just mentioned, the critical reliance of the whole society upon each harvest had long justified government control of everything from the working of the land to the times and places where grain might be sold. Such a well-defined set of economic obligations clearly formed a system that was social in origin, but with the increase in free exchanges, observers began to construe the voluntary but uniform acts of market participants as elements in a natural system. The new economic relations were undirected but patterned, uncoerced but orderly, free but predictable. They began to resemble—in men's minds at least—the operation of systems in the physical universe. Locating the ordering mechanism for this system in the consistent drive of individuals to seek their advantage, writers began talking about it as natural, often invoking, as Davenant did, the natural law of self-preservation. I must say that I still find this a very puzzling conclusion. Even a perfectly free global economy would rely upon social conventions and legal processes in countless ways. In fact, international law developed in response to world trade. I can only surmise that the intellectual categories of early modern thinkers were too dichotomic, too either/or, to permit a more refined judgement. The novel uniformities in the expanding market economy outshone the more familiar diversity. Men and women were acting voluntarily, yet their responses produced consistent results. This suggested the force of nature. As more and more goods and payments crossed national boundaries, the political power within each state seemed less and less relevant to the system as whole. Indeed, as commercial bargains extended through time and

8. Charles Davenant, "A Memorial Concerning the Coyn of England," 1695, in Abbott Payson Usher, ed., *Two Manuscripts by Charles Davenant* (Baltimore, 1942).

space they became less subject to the influence of place, persons, and prescribed usages, those powerful arbiters of premodern society.

The most subversive aspect of this imaginative model of the economy was the implication that government supervision of the economy was not only unwarranted, but ineffective, much like a statute against floods and earthquakes. Many pamphleteers did reach that conclusion. John Locke wrote dogmatically that it would be impossible "by any contrivance of law to prevent men from getting money" at whatever rate they were willing to pay.[9] The new commentary about natural economic relations intruded upon a world still dominated by habit and authority, but it was an idea whose champions would increase in number. Although Europe remained robustly Christian, the idea of a natural economic system was like an entering wedge between God and His created universe. The further it moved into popular consciousness the more tenuous became the connection between divine will and mundane outcomes. Providence was still invoked to explain remarkable events while the round of activities that composed everyday life succumbed to purely secular explanations. The reconceptualization of economic life came at a time when nature and science were also being redefined. Again, venerable terms acquired new meanings. The medieval natural law of conscience and right reason took on the modern sense of natural law as cause and effect. Without clearly distinguishing between the two senses it was possible to attach to the new scientific natural law the moral coloration of natural laws enjoined by God.[10] From this fusion we get such ambiguous but evocative concepts as "nature's God" and inalienable rights, which convey both moral and factual affirmations.

The economists' model of human nature that took shape in seventeenth-century English writings can be compared to a laser beam. Broad illumination was traded for intense

9. [John Locke], *Some Considerations of the Consequences of the Lowering of Interest* (London, 1692), pp. 1–2.

10. William Letwin, *The Origins of Scientific Economics* (London, 1983), pp. 147–48.

scrutiny. The variety of human expressions that engaged poets, satirists, and theologians were left in the shadows, while the desires that made men and women work harder and found fulfillment in sales and purchases were counted, measured, and analyzed. *Homo faber,* man the doer, took precedence in these writings over man the believer, man the contemplator, even man the sinner. When work was no longer seen as part of an unending drudgery that just kept people alive, it took on a new value. Work created surpluses for exchange; work created wealth. In reevaluating work, those who marveled at the world's new productivity were enhancing the worth of labor—what ordinary men and women did. In the seventeenth century also began that stream of improvement tracts that has never ceased to flow from Western presses—descriptions of how to reclaim wastelands, link up rivers with canals, thresh wheat and, yes, build better mousetraps. The prospect of prosperity also called forth the vision of a functioning society. No less a sober thinker than John Locke confided on a scrap of foolscap, still among his papers, the visionary hope that if everyone in the world had to work every day, the world's work could be done with just a half a day's labor. Amusing as that may seem, it reveals the dawning awareness that God's curse on Adam to labor by the sweat of his brow might in fact be lifted by man's own inventiveness. In these random, even trivial, observations we get a glimpse of the homogenizing effect of the study of economic activities upon men who had been born into a highly inflected society. The fixed hierarchy of social statuses that formed so visible a part of early modern life was being challenged, if only in the imagination, by the implications of a voluntarily integrated economy.

Opportunities for enterprise grew at a much more rapid rate than the capacity of government to oversee them and quite ordinary men were initiating many of the new trade connections and production schemes. Free choice and freedom of action were becoming more conspicuous in daily life. Indirectly we can see the consequences of this in the political theories of Hobbes and Locke. Unlike most of their con-

temporaries they thought it necessary to ground civil society
in the free consent of men rather than upon dominion or
God's command. Though very different, both of their theories offer an explanation of why men would consent to put
themselves under a government, why they would contract
with one another as a means of forming themselves into
civil society. Bertrand de Jouvenal once commented that social contract theories "are the views of childless men who
must have forgotten their childhood." He is making of
course the same point that Hobbes's contemporary made
when he accused Hobbes of forgetting that life begins with
children's dependence upon their parents.[11] We have a nice
juxtaposition here of the traditional and the liberal. The
traditionalist begins with the person as a member of society
born into a complex of obligations and identities, whereas
the liberal analyst starts with the individual who possesses a
common set of needs. Locke and Hobbes had not forgotten
their childhoods. Rather they had the prescience to realize
that one's childhood was becoming less important—from a
political point of view—than one's autonomy as an adult.

As more and more men and women sold their labor or
the product of their land, they became parts of a process of
producing goods for distant markets. The rewarding system
of commerce then intruded upon customary ways of distributing wealth. The market reached through the old group-
ings of town, guild, and family to the single individual. When
the market economy was examined, its inner dynamic was
located in an internal drive within each person. Thus both
actual experiences with commerce and the model used to
explain its workings eroded the ties of community. The organic conception of the whole in which the sum remains
greater than its parts began losing ground to the idea of the
whole as the sum of the parts. Hobbes and Locke started
with the individual's interest in forming civil society. They
let slip from sight the venerable notion of a community
which represented values and traditions that could not be

11. Bertrand de Jouvenel, *The Pure Theory of Politics* (Cambridge, 1963), p.
232.

reduced to the discrete and particular aims of individual members.

Commerce was dissolving restraints upon competition and unlinking old dependencies. As it did so a new reality was being created for English men and women. The reality itself was the result of historical developments, many of them very specific to those people living in the northwest corner of Europe and some colonial outposts in the New World. Yet when men began to analyze this new reality they generalized about the situation and spoke in terms of the universal qualities of trade and the uniform character of human participants. Like Hobbes's and Locke's theory of the origins of government, their model of the economy was rationalistic. It was built up from general propositions rather than composed from empirical evidence derived from historical example. Because they chose to view this novel economic behavior as universal, they could claim that it was natural as well.

The evident influence of self-interest in men's dealings had yet another impact upon old ideas. Traditional political thought emphasized the transcendent importance of the common good. Serving the common good gave a moral end to government. James Harrington drew upon classical texts—what he called ancient prudence—to demonstrate the connection between social stability and civic virtue. Property, he stressed, gave men the independence to place the common weal above their private concerns. But even as Harrington's classical republican ideals were gaining ground among the English ruling class, others were beginning to be skeptical about the whole idea of there even being a common good. Matthew Wren, for instance, maintained that Harrington had never proved its existence. The central question, Wren wrote in a critique of Harrington, was whether there was a common right or interest more excellent than that of the parts. Harrington, he noted, had offered no proof—only other authorities. Wren also questioned that any distribution of landed property could secure stability, the yearning for which had become more acute among Englishmen as the necessary condition for it became less likely to prevail.[12]

Both Wren's assertions that there was no general interest and that the fluidity of wealth precluded a stabilizing distribution of property reflected the changing economic structure in England. Men's perceptions of their particular interests had grown stronger because of the constant permutations of values produced in a commercial society. As the ambit of economic freedom and international trade widened, those entrusted with political power could no longer control the creation and distribution of wealth within their own societies. They might, however, use government to secure economic privileges for themselves and thereby insinuate into politics that dynamic of self-interest that animated the market. Just as the limited agricultural productivity of an earlier age justified the authoritarian oversight of social life, so the expectations unleashed by commercial growth subtly predisposed people to act and think along more liberal lines.

Ideas about sovereignty, the common good, proper conduct, and social purposes in general cannot be reduced to economic conditions, but there is a close connection between reality and conceptions of reality. We can expect them to exert a reciprocal influence. When new notions about civil society and human nature were put into circulation because mundane experience in late seventeenth-century England had changed, we are given a rare glimpse of the formation of an ideology. That the analytical commentary about the market and human behavior appeared so close to the actual economic changes shows us how novelties goad the imagination. It also indicates how the human need to comprehend experience finds expression in descriptions which lead to new depictions of reality. If the eighteenth century was an ideological age it is because economic developments were unsettling old understandings. Since these old understandings embraced not only politics and economics but deeply held convictions about human purpose as well, those who

12. [Matthew Wren], *Considerations on Mr. Harrington's Common-wealth of Oceana* (London, 1657), pp. 20–22, 88–89.

cherished venerable beliefs were prepared to offer stiff opposition to the champions of change. The latter's success was not, however, determined solely by the quality of the ideas. The relative power of conservatives and innovators to control other people's lives, if not their actual thinking, influenced the outcome, and since this power emerged from specific social situations, we should not be surprised to find that in America the debate over economic realities was different from that in England.

During the course of the eighteenth century more and more English capital flowed to the colonies—directly in investments in the colonial economy, indirectly through the extension of credit to colonists who themselves responded to the incentives of the burgeoning Atlantic trade by bringing more land into cultivation, increasing their surplus production, and buying labor in the form of slaves and servants. Despite a relatively high rate of natural increase the demand for labor outstripped the supply and every colony continued to import people through the course of the eighteenth century. Unlike Europe with its underemployed poor, the colonies exhibited the remarkable phenomenon of a society experiencing rapid population growth without a decline in the standard of living. Instead of pressing upon the means of subsistence, Americans pressed upon fertile land. This was particularly the case after 1750 when European immigrants and internal migrants began moving through Western Pennsylvania, Virginia, and Maryland into the back country.[13]

Prosperity in a commercial economy is always subject to abrupt arrests. Tobacco gluts had plagued the Tideland planters of the South from the earliest days of settlement. Good times in the Northern colonies were paced by the fluctuating profits of the West Indian sugar planters who were their best customers. England's war expenditures, especially the outfitting of her fleets, added boom and bust

13. Marc Egnal, "The Economic Development of the Thirteen Continental Colonies, 1720 to 1775," *William and Mary Quarterly,* 32 (1975), 191–222; and Robert D. Mitchell, *Commercialism and Frontier: Perspectives on the Early Shenandoah Valley* (Charlottesville, 1977), pp. 173–78.

cycles to other rhythmic oscillations in the colonial economy. Through much of the colonial period these sudden changes in the volume and profitability of market exchanges principally affected townfolk and the planters of the staple-growing South. In the middle of the eighteenth century a significant shift in international demand brought more and more American farmers into the market. Europeans were beginning to run out of food, a fact of considerable importance to the economic prospects of ordinary colonists. After a century of stagnation, population began to grow again in Europe—in fact, worldwide. England, which had been a major exporter of grains, had barely enough food to feed its growing population. Other European countries, especially Spain and Portugal, that had not adopted harvest-enhancing improvements, felt the pinch even more keenly. The demand for food expressed itself most obviously in higher grain prices. After 1757 the terms of trade changed decisively in favor of grain. A bushel of wheat commanded more and more in manufactured goods and labor. Its price had doubled by the end of the century and would rise half against as much more before it peaked in the great European famine year of 1818–19.[14]

The rise in grain prices translated itself in America into a sustained incentive to produce for this European market. For planters in the upper South this involved more intense cropping in order to grow both tobacco and wheat. By the time of the Revolution, many Virginia and Maryland planters, large and small, had switched to grain. Elsewhere in the great grain-growing arc that rose from the James River through the middle states to the Connecticut River Valley, rising food prices encouraged family farmers to raise a larger surplus while commercial millers and grain merchants went further and further inland for the harvests to ship abroad. By 1789, when the first federal government under the new constitution was assembling, the promise of prosperity had

14. B.H. Slicher Van Bath, "Eighteenth Century Agriculture on the Continent of Europe: Evolution or Revolution?" *Agricultural History*, 43 (1969), 174–75. See also the record of British wheat imports from the United States in Great Britain, *Parliamentary Papers* (Commons), "An Account of the Grain of All Sorts, Meal, and Flour, Stated in Quarters, Imported into Great Britain in Each Year from January 5, 1800 to January 5, 1825" (no. 227), 1825, 20, 233–67.

not only materialized but the dominance of the grain trade had significantly altered the character of commerce in the new American nation.[15]

The most obvious change was the escalating demand for the crops that small family farms produced. Instead of duplicating the grains that all European countries raised, American food and fibers now possessed a strong commercial value. The increase of population that mounted steadily through the eighteenth century created shortfalls in food everywhere. England, which had previously helped supply the deficiencies in the staff of life in Portugal and Spain, virtually withdrew from the grain trade. In 1789 a British committee of trade reported that England could expect future shortage in all of the grains save barley. For 27 out of the next 30 years Britain did in fact import wheat and flour, reaching out frequently beyond the Baltic breadbasket to North America.[16]

The commercial value of the ordinary farmer's surplusses undergirt a new prosperity in the North and blurred the old textbook distinction between the Southern staple-growing agriculture and the Northern direct consumption rural economy. During the first quarter-century of independence, Northern states for the first time passed Southern ones in per capita wealth. By the 1790s the North accounted for more than half of all United States exports. The surge in international trade in the foods and fibers grown on typical American farms outside the Tidewater South brought the country out of the post-revolutionary depression.[17] While prospering from the demand for wheat, corn, salt meat, flour, biscuits, beeswax, flax and hemp, the farmers did not need to change their way of life. They could augment

15. *Eighty Years' Progress of the United States from the Revolutionary War to the Great Rebellion* (Springfield, Ma., 1864), pp. 136–41; Stanley L. Engerman, "A Reconsideration of Southern Economic Growth, 1770–1860," *Agricultural History*, 69 (1975), 348–49; Carville Earle and Ronald Hoffman, "Staple Crops and Urban Development in the Eighteenth-Century South," *Perspectives in American History*, 10 (1976); and Paul G. E. Clemens, *From Tobacco to Grain* (Ithaca, 1981).

16. Hubert G. Schmidt, "Some Post-Revolutionary Views of American Agriculture in the English Midlands," *Ibid.*, 32 (1958), p. 173; and "An Account of the Grain," *Parliamentary Papers* (Commons), no. 227, 1825.

17. Thomas Jefferson, *Notes on the State of Virginia*, William Peden, ed. (Chapel Hill, 1955), pp. 166–68.

the labor of their families at harvest time and the mixed husbandry that best protected soil fertility called for the diversification of cropping rather than specialization.

It is hard to gauge the extent of agricultural improvements in America. There was a surge of interest among gentlemen farmers. What foreign visitors noticed was the ease of the American farmer's life. With much larger holdings than those among the European peasantry and a relatively low level of taxation, American farmers did not have to labor long hours. In his *Notes on the State of Virginia,* Jefferson attributed to wheat raising the moral benefits singularly missing from tobacco, "a culture productive of infinite wretchedness." The cultivation of wheat was the reverse in every circumstance, Jefferson said, because "it feeds the labourers plentifully, requires from them only moderate toil, except at harvest, and diffuses plenty and happiness among the whole." This benign conception of an economy of food production was to have far-reaching ideological implications. The first and most striking one was the association of America's prosperity with free labor—the free and independent labor of farmer-owners and their families. Although slaves labored in the wheat and corn fields throughout the Piedmont and upper South, the imagery evoked was of the family farm in happy contrast to the 'infinite wretchedness' of slave-worked staple plantations. In that interlude between the wartime destruction of tobacco, indigo, and rice and the spectacular bonanza in cotton, the food-producing farm actually and imaginatively embodied the promise of American agriculture. Its cornucopian abundance acquired moral significance because it was tied to the real needs of people everywhere. As Paine had written in *Common Sense,* America would always flourish, as long as "eating is the custom of Europe." The solidity of the demand for food nurtured the illusion that the American economy was based on fundamental needs, unlike that of England and France, where manufacturing produced gewgaws for the rich and debased living conditions for the poor.[18]

18. Thomas Paine, *Common Sense, The Writings of Thomas Paine,* Moncure Daniel, ed. (Conway, N.Y., 1894–96), I, 86.

Marketing food crops in America, even during the colonial period, had created a host of ancillary trades. Millers, teamsters, ship and wagon builders, bakers, coopers, and grain merchants sprang up to process, transport, and sell American grains. Where tobacco planters converted to wheat in the upper South urban networks appeared. Baltimore was but the most conspicuous example of a city built on grain. Throughout the 1790s the population of Pennsylvania and New York—the centers of both the raising and marketing of foodstuffs—grew by 60 percent, while that of the rest of the nation increased only 25 to 35 percent. The compatability of food raising with a wide range of urban trades created a sense of the mutuality of economic interests. When Albert Gallatin, as a congressman from western Pennsylvania, protested the Federalists' Bankruptcy Act of 1800, he did so on the grounds that its benefits were restricted to merchants when in fact in America, according to him, the different professions and trades were blended together in the same person, "the same man being frequently a farmer and a merchant, and perhaps a manufacturer." Based as it was upon the hunger of a growing population, this economy appeared natural and uncoerced. It did not require bounties for its promotion, nor need it be protected with tariffs. Fundamental, universal, and comprehensive, America's burgeoning commerce in foodstuffs became exemplary of the harmony of free economic relations. A growing consensus developed that government, as Alexander Dallas put it, should "let commerce flow in its own natural channels." [19]

The pervasiveness of wheat growing in America also created common interests among the states in the new nation. Climate and soil fertility excluded parts of New En-

19. Earle and Hoffman, "Staple Crops and Urban Development;" *Annals of the Congress,* 5 Cong. 3 sess., Jan. 14, 1799, 2650–51; and [Alexander James Dallas], *Features of Mr. Jay's Treaty* (Philadelphia, 1795), pp. 21–22. An increase in demand for whiskey extended the grain-based prosperity to the back country where Alexander Addison, the presiding judge of the 5th judicial district of Pennsylvania reported in 1794 that the progress of wealth had been amazingly rapid, noting the lowest number of sheriff sales in nine years and the appearance of a dozen of burr millstones in an area where three years ago there had been none, as cited in Jacob E. Cooke, "The Whiskey Insurrection: A Re-evaluation," *Pennsylvania History,* 30 (1963), 334.

gland and the Tidewater South from this form of commercial agriculture, but the rest of the nation participated, including the farmers taking up the new lands of the West. They did not need each other, but they shared a set of concerns about taxation, transportation, access to credit, outlets to the Atlantic trade lanes, and commercial treaties. Perhaps as important as these concrete issues, they were open to a similar conception of the social order. Because the rising prices in foodstuffs was paralleled in the 1790s with the availability of good arable land in western Pennsylvania, New York, Virginia, and Maryland, and the new territories of Kentucky and Tennessee, the prospects of prosperity in the grain trade could be linked with opportunity for each man to make his own way on his own terms with his own initiative. In New York, where tenantry had been the most apparent in the colonial period, all new lands after independence were granted in fee simple by the Land Office.[20] The poor landless man—be he immigrant or young American-born—who took up his own land and assumed the roles of father, farmer, citizen, and officeholder, became a staple figure in July 4th oratory. The ease of subsistence, a Republican proclaimed in 1793, "recommends this quarter of the globe to the poor everywhere," going on to claim that with the abundance of employment and high wages "a prudent man in a few years may lay up enough to purchase a farm in one of the newly settled towns [and] maintain a family with ease." Typical too was the editorial commentary in the Newark *Centinel of Freedom* following a letter on the misery of the Irish cottager: "No wonder so many come to this Land of Comfort, where, blessed with health and being industrious, no one needs despair of a comfortable livelihood at least." The rapidity of settlements in Vermont astounded others. "Large tracts of land which two or three years past

20. Julius Rubin, "The Limits of Agricultural Progress in the Nineteenth-Century South," *Agricultural History*, 49 (1975); Claudia D. Goldin and Frank D. Lewis, "The Role of Exports in American Economic Growth during the Napoleonic Wars, 1793 to 1807," *Explorations in Economic History*, 17 (1980); Alfred F. Young, *The Democratic Republicans of New York: The Origins, 1763–1797* (Chapel Hill, 1967), pp. 234–39; and Samuel Latham Mitchell, *An Oration before the Society of Black Friars* (New York, 1793), pp. 19–20.

were nothing more than an uncultivated wilderness now teem with vegetation, nurtured by the industrious hand of agriculture. The axe of the husbandman has made bare the forest, and fields of grain supply the place of lofty trees. In short the face of nature throughout every part of that district has a much more pleasant appearance, and gives us an idea of the future greatness of this young but rising empire."[21]

Louis Hacker noted thirty years ago that there had always been an anticapitalist bias in the writing of American history. The reason for this is not hard to find. Historians began discussing capitalism as a specific economic system in the early twentieth century, when the ugliness of American industrialization obtruded everywhere. Capitalists themselves appeared as plutocrats grinding the faces of the poor with one hand while subverting the democratic institutions of the nation with the other. The great concentrations of wealth lodged in the "dark satanic mills" of industry made a mockery of equality of opportunity and the older justification for limiting government interference lost its liberal rationale. Capitalist apologists drew instead upon the grim determinism of the Social Darwinian doctrine of the survival of the fittest.[22]

When historians in the early twentieth century began to examine seriously the influence of economic factors in the American past, they appeared as independent developments, the characteristics of which were established with free enterprise. Capitalism figured in historical texts then as an entity—an organic object—like an oak whose form was determined with the planting of the first acorn. Rather than imagine different groups of people in the eighteenth century responding selectively to the possibilities afforded by the market, scholars wrote about capitalism as an external force bending men and nations to its needs. Both the anticapitalist bias that Hacker commented upon and this con-

---

21. *Ibid.*, pp. 21–22; *Massachusetts Centinel*, September 15, 1784. See also April 10, 1784 for a contemporary's report on the rapidity of town formation on the western frontier.

22. F.A. Hayek, ed., *Capitalism and the Historians* (London, 1954), pp. 85–87.

cept of capitalism as an independent system have obscured the role that the expectation of commercial growth played in the social thought of the Jeffersonian Republicans. Instead the hard-fisted, mean-spirited drive for profits of early industrialization seemed so totally incompatible with Jeffersonian ideals that historians construed the Jeffersonians themselves as anticapitalistic. Similarly, the tendency to see industrial capitalism as the end toward which all prior economies were moving has contributed to the notion that those in the past who promoted agriculture were out of touch with the progressive developments of their day.[23]

A number of findings of the past generation have made it possible to look anew at capitalism as it appeared to men and women at the end of the eighteenth century. It is now generally recognized that the first capitalists were farmers and landlords—the men who revolutionized English agriculture in the seventeenth and eighteenth centuries. Far from being the stronghold of conservatism, the countryside witnessed dramatic changes in the working and holding of land. The breakthrough in agricultural productivity not only freed the English from famine; it liberated their imagination as well. With old assumptions undermined, radical theories about individual freedom acquired plausibility. In England and America commercial farming was a progressive economic force suggesting to some that the future would be far different from the past. But, equally important, we now know that these advances occurred in some countries and not others, despite similar physical characteristics. No such breakthrough, for instance, took place in France. Indeed the Physiocrats' enthusiasm for agricultural improvements and free trade represented as much as anything a longing

---

23. The classic version of this statement can be found in Richard Hofstadter, *The Age of Reform* (New York, 1955), pp. 23–24, 30, and Vernon Parrington, *Main Currents of American Thought* (New York, 1927–30), vol. 3, xxvii–iii. For more recent restatements see J.G.A. Pocock, "Virtue and Commerce in the Eighteenth Century," *Journal of Interdisciplinary History*, 3 (1972), 134; Lance Banning, *The Jeffersonian Persuasion* (Ithaca, 1978), p. 269; and Drew R. McCoy, *The Elusive Republic* (Chapel Hill, 1980), p. 10. A nice corrective to this view can be found in John Zvesper, *Political Philosophy and Rhetoric: A Study of the Origins of American Party Politics* (Cambridge, 1977), pp. 12–13.

to replicate the miracle of abundance across the Channel.[24] Clearly, political decisions and the subtler influences of culture were at work in producing these different economic outcomes. Instead of capitalism impressing itself upon a passive nation or, as in Adam Smith's explanation, the division of labor leading inexorably to economic development, the history of European people on both sides of the Atlantic indicates that responsiveness to the market economy cannot be taken for granted, for it reflects values and ideas even more than material conditions.

In recent work on late eighteenth-century America scholars have begun to explore the connection between the economy and the cultural milieu in which commercial engagements took place. In doing this they are building upon an impressive body of recent scholarship detailing the character and structure of everyday life. By itself this work has forced a reevaluation of the validity of Adam Smith's model of human nature, that is, the appetitive, rationalistic, propulsively self-improving economic man who stands at the center of the theory that has come to dominate modern Western thinking about the market economy. Working within the conceptual framework Charles Beard pioneered seventy years ago, Jackson Turner Main, for instance, has examined the economic forces at play in the 1780s in a way that does justice to their capacity to shape the actual social experience of Americans and through those recurring and commonplace events create the values and attitudes that become encoded in culture. First identifying a cluster of issues that consistently divided legislators, Main worked back to the constituencies that elected the legislators and discovered that American voters were either localists or cosmopolitans, depending upon whether they lived in Western areas or along the Atlantic seaboard. As the labels suggest, the lives of localists were narrowly confined while cosmopolitans responded to a bigger and wealthier world enlarged by trade, education, and access to Europe. Tracing political divisions

24. Elizabeth Fox-Genovese, *The Origins of Physiocracy* (Ithaca, 1976), pp. 98–100; and Andrew B. Appleby, "Grain Prices and Subsistence Crises in England and France, 1590–1740," *Journal of Economic History*, 39 (1979).

back to the communities from which various legislators came, Main has been able to show that the degree of commercial involvement directly affected the sophistication of the voters and their representatives. Thus economics exerted its influence more through the quality of everyday encounters than through one's place in the market system. Main's categories are true to eighteenth-century reality, for they take into account the fact that in a world not yet thoroughly modern the kind of community men and women lived in frequently influenced their choices more than their membership in a particular social group within the community.[25]

Main's analysis can also be used to shed light on the striking regional concentrations of Federalists and Jeffersonians a decade later when the promise of prosperity superseded the depressed outlook of the post-revolutionary period. The upturn in trade that coincided with the adoption of the Constitution and the rising demand for the foods and fibers grown by ordinary farmers in the wheat belt greatly increased the commercial penetration of the market throughout the 1790s. The Northern centers for growing and marketing grains then increased at twice the rate of the rest of the nation and the number of Main's cosmopolitan towns grew apace. Even Massachusetts counties that had no cosmopolitan towns in the 1780s acquired several in the 1790s. The spectacular growth in the middle states was accompanied by true prosperity. The real value of wages, profits, and land all rose substantially. The strength of the Jeffersionian movement was precisely in the fast-growing areas. As individuals, the Jeffersonians were socially and geographically mobile, particularly in the North. They were the mushroom candidates that the established political leaders scorned. In studies discriminating between new and old wealth, Jeffersonian towns are distinguished by the recentness of their money. Republicans succeeded where entrenched elites were challenged by new men, but they flour-

25. Jackson Turner Main, *Political Parties before the Constitution* (Chapel Hill, 1973). See also Van Beck Hall, *Politics Without Parties: Massachusetts, 1780–1791* (Pittsburgh, 1972). Beard's ideas can be traced in his *Economic Origins of Jeffersonian Democracy* (New York, 1927).

ished as well without opposition in young cities like Baltimore.[26]

In the 1790s the newness of profitable enterprise in many places and the rapidity of growth elsewhere created a division between the mobile and the established that was similar to Main's split between locals and cosmopolitans. Again it is the kinds of experiences that mobility and stability promoted that counted, but the content of Republican ideology cannot be derived solely from a social category. Federalists and Republicans alike responded to the economic opportunities opening before America. After all, it was Federalist Gouverneur Morris who hailed his countrymen as "the first-born children of the commercial age," and the runaway winner in grandiose land speculation was Manasseh Cutler, a conservative Massachusetts clergyman.[27] Where Republicans differed from Federalists was in the moral character they gave to economic development. The promise in prosperity encouraged them to vault over the cumulative wisdom of the ages and imagine a future far different from the dreary past known to man. In taking this imaginative leap they were greatly aided by the line of economic analysis that began with English writers in the seventeenth century and culminated in Adam Smith's *Wealth of Nations*. The uniformity of economic responses from market participants,

26. Frank A. Cassell, "The Structure of Baltimore's Politics in the Age of Jefferson, 1795–1812," in Aubrey C. Land et al., eds., *Law, Society, and Politics in Early Maryland* (Baltimore, 1977), pp. 279–82. See also Edwin Gwynne Burrows, "Albert Gallatin and the Political Economy of Republicanism, 1761–1800" (Columbia University dissertation, 1974), pp. 245ff.; Young, *Democratic Republicans of New York,* pp. 581–82; Thomas Lawrence Davis, "Aristocrats and Jacobins in Country Towns: Party Formation in Berkshire County, Massachusetts (1775–1816)" (Boston University dissertation, 1975), vi, pp. 183–84, where Davis discusses the upward mobility and commercial advance in Republican towns in comparison to Federalist ones; Edmund Philip Willis, "Social Origins of Political Leadership in New York City from the Revolution to 1815" (University of California, Berkeley dissertation, 1967), pp. 132–36, 160–61; and Paul Goodman, "Social Status of Party Leadership: The House of Representatives, 1797–1804," *William and Mary Quarterly,* 25 (1968), 474.

27. Gouverneur Morris to Matthew Ridley, August 6, 1782, as cited in Clarence Ver Steeg, *Robert Morris: Revolutionary Financier* (Philadelphia, 1954), pp. 166–67; and Joseph Stancliffe Davis, *Essays in the Earlier History of American Corporations* (Cambridge, Ma., 1917), pp. 136–42.

which had encouraged a succession of observers to think of social relations as a complex of exchanges between similarly rational and self-interested bargainers, pushed the Jeffersonians even further toward nineteenth-century liberalism. In England conspicuous social distinctions worked against acceptance of the economists' model as a depiction of reality, whereas the more equal social conditions that prevailed in America made it possible to think of the economists' description of the market as a template for society. What in England served as a device for understanding how nations grow wealthy through trade became in America the blueprint for a society of economically progressive, socially equal, and politically competent citizens. Capitalism thus disclosed itself in a benign and visionary way to Republicans who drew from its dynamic operation the promise of a new age for ordinary men.

A Vision
of Classlessness

"IN AGES of equality every man naturally stands alone," Alexis de Tocqueville concluded after his tour of America in 1831, going on to explain that the man in an age of equality "has no hereditary friends whose cooperation he may demand—no class upon whose sympathy he may rely." In the introduction to his great study, *Democracy in America*, Tocqueville said that nothing had struck him more forcibly than the general equality of condition in the United States. To it he attributed the paradoxical self-reliance and powerlessness of the individual in America. At once capable of taking care of himself without reference to any authority, the single citizen was impotent before the collective will of the majority. In order to make these points about the effect of equality upon the character of social life, Tocqueville created a foil against which to examine democracy. It was aristocracy. Aristocratic institutions, he maintained, had the effect of closely binding every man to several of his fellow citizens. In aristocratic communities all occupied fixed positions, one above the other, the result being that each man always sees someone above himself whose patronage is necessary to him and below him another man whose cooperation he may claim.[1]

The central feature of Tocqueville's idealized version

1. Alexis de Tocqueville, *Democracy in America*, Henry Reeve, ed., revised by Phillips Bradley (New York, 1949), 2, 342–43; 1, 1.

of aristocracy was the presence of an organic solidarity in
society. The most common metaphor used to evoke this solidarity was that of the body politic. Like the human body, it
was said, society drew its health from the diverse organs or
ranks, hierarchically arranged, which functioned for the
common good. Thus diversity, inequality, dependency—even
special privileges—played their part. Above all, the interests
of the individual, or more appropriately, the single member
of society, were subordinated to the whole. It was the whole
that sustained the individual, not vice versa. "Aristocracy,"
Tocqueville said, "had made a chain of all the members of
the community, from the peasant to the king: democracy
breaks that chain, and severs every link of it."[2] The chain
he spoke of also tied men and women to specific locales and
linked them to a lineal family, a rank, an occupation, a re-
gion. In many ways this conception of organic society re-
sembled that famous egg, Humpty Dumpty. Once it was
broken not all the king's horses nor all the king's men could
put it back together again.

Americans, particularly in New England, had built
strong communities, but the dislocations of the revolution
and movement on to new land had uprooted many while
population growth and immigration acted constantly to undermine their sense of settledness. Had Tocqueville visited
the United States a generation earlier he would have en-
countered his organic ideal operating variously as a goal, as
a reality, and as a set of discordant values. He would not
then have been able to ascribe the democratic character of
American culture to something as inert and lifeless as the
general equality of condition, for he would have witnessed

2. *Ibid.*, 2, 105. Without the scholarship of the past score of years we would
not now be in possession of the essential details of the nurtured communities of
colonial America. For astute and contentious views on the significance of the organic traditions planted in that period, see James A. Henretta, "Families and Farms:
Mentalité in Pre-Industrial America," *William and Mary Quarterly*, 35 (1978); James
T. Lemon, "The Weakness of Place and Community in Early Pennsylvania," in
James R. Gibson, ed., *European Settlement and Development in North America* (Toronto, 1978); *idem.*, "Communications, with a Reply by James A. Henretta," *William and Mary Quarterly*, 37 (1980); and Richard R. Beeman, "The New Social History and the Search for 'Community' in Colonial America," *American Quarterly*, 29
(1977).

the process through which the new nation shed its bor-
rowed European ethos. In the 1790s the aristocratic model
of society was isolated and attacked. Those who experienced it as a set of discordant values faced those who knew
it as a reality and an ideal. In this chapter I will look at the
events and responses that made the attackers successful. I
will concentrate upon the writings and speeches of the political newcomers of the middle states, for they were the ones
who turned a congressional party based in the South into a
great popular movement drawing its strength from the ordinary voters in the center of the Union.

When Jefferson arrived in New York City in 1790 to
take up his duties as Secretary of State in George Washington's first administration, he confided in his journal his shock
at the aristocratic sympathies he soon discovered. Quick to
be included in the official social life that Federalist hostesses
had created during the sessions of Congress, Jefferson was
dismayed by the manners and sentiments evident at the dinner parties he attended. He was, he said, the only advocate
of the republican side in debates, "unless, among the guests,
there chanced to be some member of that party from the
legislative Houses."[3] Jefferson's fulminations were more an-
ticipatory than typical. They help us understand, however,
why he was ready to put himself at the head of the common
man's cause when it materialized. In tone and substance his
complaints differed from the criticism of administration
policies that had surfaced in the very first session of Congress. In these disputes, which were prompted largely by
the boldness with which Alexander Hamilton had asserted

3. Thomas Jefferson, "Anas," in Paul Leicester Ford, ed., *The Writings of Thomas
Jefferson* (New York, 1892–1899), vol. 1, 160. A less than enthusiastic but nonetheless perceptive editor, Paul Leicester Ford, commented in the introduction to the
Autobiography of Thomas Jefferson, 1743–1790 (New York, 1914), xiii–xv, that "Unlike the Federalists, Jefferson was willing to discard the tradition of ages—that the
people must be protected against themselves by the brains, money and better 'elements' of the country—and for this reason American democracy made him its
chosen agent and mouth-piece. Inheriting unsettling tendenceis of mind, he was
from an early age a thorough skeptic of tradition and precedent. In his own words,
he never 'feared to follow truth and reason to whatever results they led, and
bearding every authority which stood in their way.'" It is exactly this quality of
Jefferson that is suppressed by enrolling him in the English Country Party.

the new federal government's financial leadership, opponents and proponents of the various measures came from the ranks of elected officials, which meant that national politics were largely confined to the activities of office holders. The genteel arena of conflict and the general agreement on the processes of law-making ensured decorum. Policy debates did not undermine the consensus among leaders on the proper relationship between government and governed people. Indeed, through the first four years under the new constitution the style, the procedures, and the personnel of Washington's administration largely fulfilled the hopes of those conservatives who had wanted to remove politics from popular influence and restore the august majesty of government.

The execution of Louis XVI in January of 1793 and the outbreak of war between France and England changed all this. Crowds all over America gathered to celebrate the early victories of the French Revolutionary army. Parades and bonfires spread the word that France had joined the United States in the world's ranks of republics. Foreign policy, that most arcane of all government responsibilities, became the major topic of public debate. Citizen Genêt's triumphal journey from Charleston to Philadelphia in April, a month after Washington's second inauguration, only advertised what had already become apparent—large portions of the American people had claimed the cause of France as their own. Washington adopted a neutrality policy designed to keep the United States from being drawn into the war, even at the cost of violating the spirit of the Franco-American treaty that had brought France into the war of American Independence. Jefferson and other administration critics within Congress recognized the wisdom of remaining neutral, but outside of government circles, neutrality was treated as a betrayal not just of France but of republican government as well. Orators at civic feasts held in honor of French victories reminded audiences that the enemies of France were "Royalists and Aristocrats associated for the express purpose of expelling the rights of Man from the world."[4] These demonstrations of support for the French Revolution were often accompanied by angry denunciations of administration policies, which were now interpreted as unwarrantedly pro-English.

This public criticism in turn precipitated a much more divisive controversy about the legality of popular participation in politics. The issue came to a head with the spontaneous formation of political organizations. Variously called democratic or republican societies, these voluntary associations sprang up in forty different locations, at least one in each state of the union. Critics blamed their appearance upon the notorious Jacobin clubs currently radicalizing French politics, but this proved to be a bite without sting in a season of revolutionary enthusiasm. Having something of a private character in Philadelphia and New York City, they become the vehicles for more turbulent, public activities elsewhere. Even in the cities they provided the nucleus for organizing ad hoc meetings. There was in this mobilization of ordinary voters the menace of numbers. Ominously from the conservatives' point of view, the democratic clubs openly attacked the forms of polite society by electing to drop conventional honorifics like "sir" and "humble servant" in favor of "fellow citizen." In further imitation of the Jacobins across the Atlantic the Democratic Society of Philadelphia resolved to measure time from the era of the Revolution. Thus their secretary dated letters "in the eighteenth year of American Independence."[5]

Clearly reckoning the general public as their own political resource, active club members reached out to one another and established correspondence across state lines. They saw to it that their resolutions and proceedings were published in each other's local newspaper, this at a time when

4. "Minutes of the Democratic Society of Pennsylvania," April 4, 1794 (Historical Society of Pennsylvania manuscript), p. 85.

5. *Ibid.*, February 22, 1794, pp. 62–63; March 8, 1794, p. 88. No less a democrat than Patrick Henry abjured the clubs and James Monroe reported from Paris that the Jacobin clubs were a bad example fo follow (Charles Downer Hazen, *Contemporary American Opinion of the French Revolution* [Baltimore, 1897], pp. 204–13).

newspapers were penetrating rural areas as never before. With several dozen voluntary clubs scrutinizing official actions and putting into circulation their invariably hostile reactions, it seemed as though the nation had acquired a second political structure competing with its government. Like kites without strings or ships without ballast, the democratic societies appeared to be alarmingly weightless to those for whom government was a heavy affair. Out of the democratic societies came the political mobilization of mere voters. The deferential quality of elections geared to choosing among virtuous candidates gave way to ones explicitly connecting men with issues instead of personal character. Newspapers in most cities became openly partisan and many towns in the middle states acquired their first journal as an outgrowth of popular interest in politics.[6]

July 4th celebrations became grand political affairs for the Federalists' opponents, their eating and drinking somewhat incongruously mingled with committee-like proceedings. The gatherers elected presidents, vice presidents, even secretaries to preside over the holiday meal and toasts with a new slate of officers installed after dinner, when resolutions were drawn up, sometimes at a second location. Those who did not attend could read the printed toasts and resolutions later in the newspaper. Liberty poles were put up and struck down as the public display of personal loyalty became a part of one's identity. Republicans, following the French again, wore red, white, and blue cockades, while Federalists responded with appropriately funereal black cockades stuck in their lapels or hatbands. Published Fourth

6. Roland M. Baumann, "Philadelphia's Manufacturers and the Excise Taxes of 1794: The Forging of the Jeffersonian Coalition," *Pennsylvania Magazine of History and Biography*, 106 (1982), 29; "Minutes of the Democratic Society," June 12, 1794, p. 117; Donald H. Stewart, *The Opposition Press of the Federalist Period* (Albany, 1969), pp. 630–31; Frank Luther Mott, *American Journalism: A History of Newspapers in the United States through 250 Years, 1690–1940* (New York, 1947), pp. 114–119. Towns that received a first newspaper in the 1790s include Chestertown, Easton, and Fredericktown, Maryland; Elizabethtown, Morristown, and Mount Pleasant, New Jersey; Catskill, Geneva, Goshen, Newburgh, Sag Harbor, Salem, and Troy, New York; and Carlisle, Chambersburg, Chestnut Hill, Greensburg, Harrisburg, Lewistown, Norristown, Northumberland, Reading, and Washington, Pennsylvania.

of July orations lost their general patriotic appeal and became part of the polemics over the meaning of republicanism. Withal the impression gained ground that the people of the United States had again been swept up in a great revolutionary force at large in the world.[7]

In this supercharged atmosphere, France and England become symbols of two alternative futures or fates for the United States: England, as the model of sober, ordered constitutional government committed to securing the maximum personal freedom consonant with the flawed nature of man, and France, presenting a vision of what a society of free men might be if the chains of customs and outworn creeds were cast off. That these opposing images were invoked in the private world of diary entries as well as the public realm of speeches suggests that more was at stake than party rhetoric. A Federalist sympathizer in rural Pennsylvania described England as "fighting the battle of the civilized world." The preservation of Great Britain was of importance to mankind because that nation had formed "the barrier betwixt the world and anarchy." No less apocalyptic was the Republican presentation of France. New Jersey toasters drank to the immortality of the principles of the Republic of France and to her success "while a despot remained." A Philadelphia resolution spoke of the sister republics of America and France as "an Hercules in the extermination of every monster of unlawful domination." Another exempted the French war from the rule of prudence guiding American neutrality because the French war would "determine whether the spirit of despotism or liberty should thereafter assume a predominating influence."[8]

The symbolic importance of France and England heightened the significance of every policy decision American officials made between 1793 and 1801. But the symbolic

7. William Cobbett complained in the *Washington Gazette*, February 4, 1797, of the popular readership of newspapers: ". . . they do read them, and thousands who read them, read nothing else."

8. [Alexander Graydon], *Memoirs of a Live, Chiefly Passed in Pennsylvania Within the Last Sixty Years* (Edinburgh, 1822), pp. 426–27; *Centinel of Freedom*, October 5, 1796; "Minutes of the Democratic Society," April 10, 1794, pp. 73–74; and *Guardian or New-Brunswick Advertiser*, July 15, 1794.

overtones were not inappropriate. The French Revolution
had succeeded in bringing to the surface of public life opposing conceptions of society. Republicans and Federalists
did not misperceive each other. Aside from flamboyant
charges of secretly conspiring to deliver the nation to a foreign power—hurled from both camps—the polemics of the
1790s clarified assumptions that had previously gone unex-
amined. It is a measure of the accuracy of the projections
from each side that no one participating in the events ever
repudiated in later years his earlier interpretation or mini-
mized the grounds for his fears. Memoirs and correspondence written in the years of retirement only confirm that
the 1790s were a decade of political passion because profound concerns had been touched. What the protracted European war did was to create a succession of occasions on
which the ardent adversaries could take one another to
task on fundamental questions about human nature and social norms.

The link between belief and action in politics is usually
left implicit. Understandings do the work of open declarations. When intellectual disputes do bubble up to the surface of public life the provocation is usually temporary. Calm
returns without too much digging among tacit assumptions.
No such reprieve came to the Federalists in power. America's diplomatic independence was at risk and the necessity
to respond to external events never abated. With England
and France turned into political models for the United
States, domestic and foreign affairs became inextricably en-
twined. The overwhelming sense of crisis forced each group
to organize for keeps. An eight-year sequence of provoca-
tive happenings sustained the ideological engagement between the Federalists and Republicans. They were pushed
to interpret the revolutionary events of their times. They
had to react to each other and they ended up defending the
philosophical underpinnings for their policy preferences. It
was a bit like pulling yarn from a skein; over time everything came out. The opposing views finally stood exposed.
To the Federalists the French Revolution was the source of
the delusions and enthusiasms that could undermine civil

order as it had been understood for generations in America. Called upon to explain this, they lay bare their fears about civil society. That they could be so explicit about the political superiority of the rich, the well-born, and the able few and so frank about the inadequacy of the ordinary many, while appealing for their votes, only reveals how commonplace these convictions had been. Federalists, however, were not mindless conservatives. Having participated in the American Revolution they warmly affirmed the freedom of self-governing, autonomous men and accepted the extended suffrage of American states. Federalists' values embraced the mobility of the meritorious—what they considered the just reward for diligence in a lawful calling—but in all essentials they remained classical republicans. Their political faith represented a modification, not a rejection, of traditional expectations about the role of authority in public life, about the permanence of social classes and the desirable distance between the governed and governors.

Unusual in any time, the Republicans' challenge to these venerable notions represented an unprecedented public exploration of the hierarchical assumptions that had dominated European thought for centuries. Nowhere else in the Western world were the conditions right for such a debate, although everywhere in Europe the questions were relevant. In France the party of reformers who had worked within the classical republican tradition in 1789 (they were appropriately called *Anglomanes* or Anglomaniacs) were decisively defeated during the first few months of the National Assembly. With every new conflict the course of the French Revolution lurched to the left until it sharply changed directions after the fall of Robespierre in 1794. Violence replaced argumentation as a way of dealing with political opposition early in the French Revolution.[9] In England on the other hand, it was agitation for changes that was ruthlessly suppressed. As the English approached the centennial of the Glorious Revolution of 1688, a parliamentary reform movement coalesced around the issues that the Americans

9. Joyce Appleby, "America as a Model for the Radical French Reformers of 1789," *William and Mary Quarterly* 28 (1971).

had raised about representation in the 1760s and 1770s. Tolerated tentatively for a few years, the escalation of violence in Paris, with the massacres of September 1792, shocked George III's ministers into action. Evocations of Locke's natural rights philosophy, attacks upon the unreformed constitution, polemical jibes at aristocratic privileges, the very existence of Thomas Paine—all menaced England's rulers. A Sedition Act in 1792 paved the way for a series of prosecutions that silenced reformers for another generation.[10]

The class bias of England's vaunted freedom of the press is well illustrated by the case of Thomas Cooper, an Englishman destined to play a central part in defining Jeffersonian positions. Cooper had been attacked by Edmund Burke on the floor of Parliament and he countered in print with a spirited salute to "the international fraternity of free peoples." The Attorney General thereupon warned him, "Continue if you please to publish your reply to Mr. Burke in an octavo form, so as to confine it probably to that class of readers who may consider it coolly: so soon as it is published cheaply," he threatened, "for dissemination among the populace, it will be my duty to prosecute."[11] Cooper heeded the warning, but more reckless reformers, particularly in Scotland, discovered the government's capacity for harshness. One man even managed to get himself arrested for reading the Magna Carta to his son.

Over the decade, England succeeded in exporting its radicals. Those convicted of sedition received transportation sentences to Australia; others fled the country at the prospect of prosecution. Tom Paine, whose *Rights of Man* plunged British authorities into a panic, went straight for the eye of the storm in Paris, but the lion's share of British political exiles made their way to Pennsylvania and New York, where their ardor for reform burned even brighter when mixed with the oxygen of toleration. No fewer than twenty played an active role in Republican politics; a dozen

10. Dumas Malone, *The Public Life of Thomas Cooper, 1783–1839* (New Haven, 1925), pp. 59–61.
11. *Ibid.*, p. 53.

of them as newspaper publishers and pamphleteers. In 1798 rebellion in Ireland led to a similar exodus. Displaying none of that hesitancy about using force evident in Boston thirty years earlier, the British government crushed the Irish uprising. Once more a contingent of English-speaking radicals found their way to the United States, leaving the unreformed English constitution safe for another generation.[12]

This comparison between France and England, on the one hand, and the United States, on the other, indicates why the debate in the 1790s about revolutionary ideals was unique. The Federalists in America had the sensibilities of the English elite but were without the power to impose them as a set of political constraints. The Jeffersonians shared many of the aspirations of the French Republicans but were without the need to destroy their conservative opponents. Instead of repression and revenge, ideological passions in the United States found an outlet in polemics and party organization. It was in fact the third time in thirty years that Americans had displayed the rather remarkable phenomenon of a people deliberating on the central propositions about government.

12. John Phillip Reid, *In a Defiant Stance: The Conditions of Law in Massachusetts Bay, the Irish Comparison, and the Coming of the American Revolution* (University Park, 1977); Richard Jerome Twomey, "Jacobins and Jeffersonians: Anglo-American Radicalism in the United States, 1790–1820" (Northern Illinois University dissertation, 1974); *idem.*, "Jacobins and Jeffersonians: Anglo-American Radical Ideology, 1790–1810," in Margaret C. Jacob and James R. Jacob, eds., *The Origins of Anglo-American Radicalism* (London, 1983); and John Hammond Moore, Theophilus Harris's Thoughts on Emigrating to America in 1793," *William and Mary Quarterly,* 36 (1979), 607n. The response of Jeffersonians to the plight of Scottish and Irish dissidents can be traced in Philip S. Foner, ed., *The Democratic-Republican Socieites, 1790–1800* (Westport, Ct., 1977), pp. 86, 414n–415n; Peter Paulson, "The Tammany Society and the Jeffersonian Movement in New York City, 1795–1800," *New York History,* 34 (1953), 82n; *The Merchants' Daily Advertiser,* July 15, 1797; *Farmers Register,* May 2, 1798; and *American Farmer and Dutchess County Advertiser,* August 1, 1799. The British expatriates in the Republican movement include James Thomas Callender, Joseph Gales, John Daly Burk, William Duane, James Cheetham, James Reynold, Denis Driscoal, Thomas Cooper, William Priestley, John Binns, Mathew Carey, John Dunlap, Donald Frazer, Matthew Lyon, Abraham Markoe, Eleazer Oswald, Hugh Henry Brackenridge, Alexander James Dallas, William Findley, John Smilie, Blair McClenachan, Aedanus Burke, and John Bingham. A Federalist writer in the Philadelphia *Gazette,* March 11, 1800, claimed that the "Jacobins" had committed the whole of their electioneering to "Cooper for Englad, Callender for Scotland and Duane for Ireland."

We can follow some of their political peregrinations through political labels. Initially the American colonists had been happy to take over the English titles Whig and Tory, especially since the favorite English classical republican authors of the patriots had dubbed themselves Real Whigs, Independent Whigs, or Honest Whigs. During the Revolution, Patriot and Loyalist became more common. The campaign for the adoption of the new constitution in 1787 witnessed the first calculated adoption of a partisan label when the proponents of the constitution disingenuously took for themselves the name Federalist. In current usage, Federalist much more clearly described the position of their hapless opponents who were stuck with the negative designation, Anti-Federalist. Still smarting from this maneuver several years later, the Anti-Federalist Elbridge Gerry suggested that since the issue had actually been over ratification it would have been more appropriate to have called the advocates of the constitution "rats" and their opponents "anti-rats." Supporters of Washington's administration retained the label Federalist once the new government was in operation. When opposition to them appeared, they tried to fix "Anti-Federalist" on their opponents, but in this they failed. James Madison referred to his congressional group as the Constitutional party; Jefferson tried to hang Oliverian on Hamilton's friends. Through all these changes, most Americans claimed to be Republicans, a term with very good connotations until the French did to Louis XVI in fact what Americans had done to George III in effigy. After 1793 those who identified with the French cause made "Republican" an odious term to conservatives. Thus, Republican finally became a party label just as the debates that swirled around the meaning of republicanism simultaneously created a national political party.[13] In doing this the Jeffersonians de-

13. Geary's statement appeared in the *Annals of the Congress*, I, 731, as cited in John Zvesper, *Political Philosophy and Rhetoric: A Study of the Origins of American Party Politics* (Cambridge, 1977), p. 29. Leonard D. White, in *The Federalists: A Study in Administration History* (New York, 1948), p. 51n, says that the Federalists took their name while defending Jay's Treaty. See also James Madison to Thomas Jefferson, April 2, 1798, in Gaillard Hunt, ed., *The Writings of James Madison* (New York, 1904), vol. 6, 313–14; Madison to James Monroe, December 4, 1794, *ibid.*,

tached the word from its classical context and made it a synonym in common usage for democracy or popular government.

At two critical junctures in 1794 the Washington administration adopted policies that enraged large segments of the American public. In both cases the vehemence of the protest caught the government unawares. Opposition to the measures swept politics out of Congress and into the cities and towns where ordinary men recast Federalist initiatives into ideological issues. This development raised the even more divisive question of how legitimate it was for the public to engage in debates about decisions that the Constitution had entrusted to duly chosen officials. As so frequently happened in the early national period, domestic controversy was triggered by a foreign event, in this case England's attack on American trading vessels. When word reached Philadelphia that the British had seized over 399 ships in the West Indies, Washington called for a build-up of American defenses. The Federalists in Congress moved to raise the excise on distilled spirits to meet the cost. The tax fell on manufactured goods as well as whiskey, but farmers west of the Alleghenies felt particularly aggrieved, because they distilled a large part of their surplus grain. Republicans, particularly political activists outside of Congress, insisted that enforcement of the excise tax was to be undertaken as a demonstration of the federal government's power. Sending revenue officers throughout the back country was, in their view, actually a vehicle for exerting authority. Already formed into democratic societies, men in western Pennyslvania offered resistance to the collection of the tax. Convinced that it was repression, not revenue, that the Federalist had in mind, they construed opposition to the

pp. 221–23; Madison to Thomas Jefferson, December 21, 1794, *ibid.*, p. 229; Thomas Jefferson, "Anas," in Ford, ed., *Writings*, I, 160; Jefferson to Stephens Thompson, October 11, 1798 in Andrew A. Lipscomb and Albert Ellery Bergh, eds., *The Writings of Thomas Jefferson* (Washington, 1905), vol. 10, 62; Christine M. Lizanich, "'The March of this Government': Joel Barlow's Unwritten History of the United States," *William and Mary Quarterly*, 33 (1976), 318–23; *Centinel of Freedom*, November 12, 1796; and broadside advertising "The American: A Country Gazette," Baltimore, November 19, 1799.

whiskey tax as a republican's duty. Thoroughly alarmed when the resistance appeared to be spreading, the Federalists called for a vigorous response. Each side played into the other's fears.[14]

When Washington led a combined state militia force of 13,000 across the mountains, the event seemed to confirm the Republicans' suspicions. The resistance to the tax actually collapsed without bloodshed, but the issue of popular participation in politics flared up with renewed heat. Many a moderate Republican repudiated the western Pennsylvanian's menacing opposition, but the Whiskey Rebellion, nonetheless, entered the pantheon of liberty's good fights. The Philadelphia Democratic Society wrangled over its inevitable resolutions for a month and the Tammany Society in New York acquired its partisan identification when moderates were outvoted by those who supported the resisters' rights. Washington himself created the occasion for further dissension when he suggested in his Congressional Address in the fall that "certain self-created societies" had been guilty of fomenting the Whiskey Rebellion.[15]

The Senate responded approvingly to Washington's speech; the House passed a watered-down censure of the resisters by one vote. But outside of Congress, Washington's effort to stigmatize popular politics clearly missed the mark as newspapers and democratic societies took up the question of what was called "the true principles of government." Members of the clubs refused to be intimidated. Advertised

14. "Minutes of the Democratic Society," pp. 127–44; Lizanich, "The March of Government," 316; *President II. Being Observations on the Late Official Address of George Washington* (Philadelphia, 1796), pp. 11–12; William Findley, *History of the Insurrection in the Four Western Counties of Pennsylvania* (Philadelphia, 1796), pp. 50–54, 75, 327; and Alexander James Dallas, "Letters on the Western Insurrection," George Mifflin Dallas Collection, box 18, folder 18, Historical Society of Pennsylvania. (Dallas, who accompanied Governor Thomas Mifflin into western Pennsylvania, confided that he had expected to find the westerners part of a "hardy, intrepid and intelligent race," but instead discovered them to be "a drunken, idle, ignorant, and perverse generation.") An interesting modern assessment of the rebellion is contained in David O. Whitten, "An Economic Inquiry into the Whiskey Rebellion of 1794," *Agricultural History*, 49 (1975).

15. Paulson, "The Tammany Society and the Jeffersonian Movement," pp. 73–77; and Rudolph M. Bell, *Party and Faction in American Politics* (Westport, Ct.), pp. 46–52.

meetings were held first in Baltimore, then Newark, Philadelphia, and New York. The 31 moderate members of the Tammany Society who had rushed through a resolution supporting Washington defended themselves by an appeal to what had once been a widely shared opinion: "The public's right to associate, speak and publish sentiments are only excellent as revolutionary means, when a government is to be overturned. An exercise of this right in a free and happy country like this," they wrote, "resembles the sport of firebrands; it is phrenzy, and this phrenzy is in proportion to the party zeal of the self-created associations."[16]

Firebrands obviously had the upper hand, for their resolution was repealed at the next general meeting. New York newspaper columnists attacked the pusillanimity of Washington's defenders. "Political associations have been threatened by the arm of power," one declared. Another claimed that duplicity or terror had induced former members to yield to Washington's condemnation. "We have erred, we have strayed like lost sheep—this is the language which your folly has suggested." When apologists for the President affirmed the right of free association, but cautioned against its use, their position was ridiculed. "What good purposes can it answer," a Republican queried, "to claim the existence of a right which you deem it criminal to exercise, and then menacingly concluded "the government that is inimical to investigation is ripe for Revolution."[17]

In this manner administration criticism of the democratic societies was turned into evidence of the government's bad intentions. The Philadelphia society stoked this particular fire, charging that the aristocratic faction in America was indefatigable in disseminating principles unfriendly to the rights of man. "It has ever been a favorite and important pursuit with aristocracy to stifle free inquiry, to envelop its proceedings in mystery, and as much as possible, to impede the progress of political knowledge. No

16. *Ibid.*, p. 49–51; "Minutes of the Democratic Society," pp. 110–16; James Madison to James Monroe, December 4, 1794, in Hunt, ed., *Writings*, 6, 220–23; Paulson, "The Tammany Society and the Jeffersonian Movement," pp. 73–74.

17. *Ibid.*; and *Independent Gazetteer*, January 24, 1795.

wonder," the resolution continued, "they were afraid of societies whose objects were to cultivate a just knowledge of
rational liberty." In a published address to their brethren,
the citizens of the United States, the New York Democratic
Society insisted that freedom of opinion had been in every
time and country the last liberty which the people have been
able to wrest from those in power.[18] The Federalist position
that democratic elections eliminated the need for informal
political associations was rejected out of hand. "In Representative Governments, the people are masters, all their officers from the highest to the lowest are servants to the people," the *Otsego Herald* proclaimed. The *Farmer's Register* of
Chambersburg, Pennsylvania, repeated the same imagery:
Legislators should always consider "that the servant is not
greater than his master, neither is he that is sent, greater
than he that sent him." Unafraid of innovation, a columnist
in Philadelphia's *Independent Gazetteer* claimed that it was in
the democratic societies that genuine republicanism had first
begun to take root. "Many of their members, undismayed
by the difficulty, turned from the specious conception of
partial form, and a Royal Republic, and set no bounds to
their zeal but in the full and entire destruction of tyranny
and the unmixed enjoyment of freedom." "For the laudable
purpose of rekindling the expiring flame of liberty have we
associated," Phineas Hedges told a July 4th audience in 1795
"not for the dark secret purposes of sedition and disorganiza-
tion which our enemies have surmised."[19]

The Federalists called upon classical republican ideas to
explain how the abuse of power should be checked within
government by the different branches of elected officers
rather than outside among a turbulent populous. But this
theory now appeared as part of elitist rhetoric. Rejecting
New Jersey Federalist Jonathan Dayton's traditional de-

18. "Minutes of the Democratic Society," pp. 110–12, 163–79; and "Address
to their Brethren, the Citizens of the United States from the New York Democratic
Society," *Independent Gazetteer*, January 21, 1795.

19. [Jedidiah Peck], *The Political Wars of Otsego* (Cooperstown, N.Y., 1796), p.
10; *Farmers' Register*, October 3, 1798; *Independent Gazetteer*, July 30, 1794; and
Phineas Hedges, *An Oration Delivered before the Republican Society of Ulster County*,
Goshen, N.Y., 1795, p. 11.

scription of the parts of government as "the constituent cen-
tinels over the liberties of the people," a Republican writer
insisted that this was not "an American conception," but
rather a notion that "favored too much the poignant principles of aristocracy." In a similar vein two rural publishers
attacked Federalist John Shippen, who had written that
freedom of the press was a blessing only "while the People
are virtuous and independent enough to check its degen-
eracy." Noting the condescension in Shippen's judgment,
they sarcastically disqualified themselves from being able to
understand "such sublime conceptions."[20]

William Findley, a Republican congressman from western Pennsylvania, readily conceded that popular meetings
led to indiscretion and promoted licentiousness. "But it does
not therefore follow," he maintained, "that such meetings
should be prohibited by law or denounced by the government." Doing so would be reducing the people to mere ma-
chines, he wrote, and subvert the very existence of liberty.
"It is the duty of the legislature not only to accommodate
the laws to the people's interests, but even as far as possible,
to their preconceptions."[21] It was not the people's wisdom
that the Republicans were arguing for, but their freedom to
err as their elected officials, they assumed, would also err.

Where classical republican theory had held up government as the noblest activity for men of civic virtue, the Jeffersonian Republicans celebrated the informal, voluntary
political life open to all. Washington's proscription of "certain self-created societies" seemed to belittle this life. "Is our
being self-created reckoned among the charges of the President?" a New Yorker asked, going on to inquire rhetorically, "Are not all private associations established on the
foundation of their own authority, an authority sanctioned
by the first principles of social life and guaranteed by the
spirit of the laws?" The logical conclusion of the Federalists'
position was finally reached by a writer in the Republican
Independent Gazetteer: "Whatever the United States might
have been previous to the American Revolution, it is pretty

20. *Independent Gazetteer*, January 28, 1795; and *Farmers' Register*, June 13, 1794.
21. Findley, *History of the Insurrection*, p. 49.

evident that since their emancipation from British rapacity, they are a great self-created society." Indeed, he continued, "had the British succeeded in impressing our minds with a firm belief in the infamy of self creation, we should never have been free and independent to all eternity."[22]

During the months that this debate raged, the terms of the treaty Jay was negotiating in England were leaked to the fiery Republican editor Benjamin Franklin Bache, aptly nicknamed Lightning Rod Jr. in reference to his grandfather. The generous concessions to Britain in the treaty represented nothing less than a sell-out to the Republicans. Again raucous public meetings became the order—or the disorder—of the day. Jay's effigy stroked the flames of many a public bonfire across the land. As one of the Philadelphia Democratic Society's resolutions explained, these events had shaken Americans from their lethargy and given new impulse and new warmth to democratic institutions.[23] They also created opportunities to explore the Federalists' pretensions of social superiority. Apparently thinking that the best offense was a good defense, Republicans enthusiastically repeated the terms of opprobrium used by Federalists. Thus one Fourth of July orator advertised that "the high prerogative set claim that the common people in this country are a set of restless, discontented, tumultuous disorganizers." Theodore Sedgwick's reference to the "ignorant herd" was linked to Edmund Burke's more notorious labeling of French commoners as the "swinish multitude." An election broadside circulated in New Jersey took the form of a deposition from a witness to a Federalist's ranting about the offense to government when common people bestir themselves in politics. "How long must government be insulted by a set of damned cut-throat Democrats?" the offender was alleged to have asked.[24] A piece in the Republi-

22. *Independent Gazetteer*, January 21, 1795 and Januray 28, 1795.

23. Morton Borden, *Parties and Politics in the Early Republic, 1789–1815* (London, 1967), pp. 47–49; and "Minutes of the Democratic Society," pp. 106–07.

24. *Centinel of Freedom*, January 25, 1797; Thomas Cooper, *Political Essays* (Philadelphia, 1800), pp. 77, 83; and *Broadside of the Republican Committee of the County of Gloucester, New Jersey, December 15, 1800*. An inflammatory English song book, "A Tribute to the Swinish Multitude," ran through three editions in New York

can *Farmer's Register* described those enlisted under the banner of democracy as "enthusiastic men, lovers of liberty, of warm passions and benevolent hearts"—hardly the qualities that commended themselves to Federalists. "If they are ignorant or dishonest, let their opponents prove it," the writer challenged.[25]

Privilege in all its forms came under attack. The Democratic Society of Washington County—the object of George Washington's attack—complained bitterly at the President's giving Chief Justice John Jay a second position as the emissary to Great Britain because it suggested that there was a "penury of virtue and talents." "No man but Washington, fenced around as he is with the unapproachable splendor of popular favor," their resolution claimed, "would have dared, in the very prime, and vigour of liberty, to have insulted the majesty of the people by such a departure from any principle of republican equality." Sending Senator James Monroe as minister to France was equally censurable. "We hold it degrading to the citizens, that it should be thought that no man can be capable of office, but one that is already thrown up, and is in some department." Popular elections, they went on to explain, showed how frequently it was a matter of accident whom the majority elects: "To suppose that those sent to the House or Senate are the only ones equal to judiciary or diplomatic trusts is a mistake, and ought to be corrected."[26] It was an outsiders' lament echoed in a Republican paper in western Massachusetts which argued that since representative republican power comes from the people, officers should be disseminated amongst the great body of the people, and men chosen "not only *of* ourselves, but as much as possibly as ourselves, Men who have the same kind of interests to protect and the same dangers to avert." Writing under the pseudonym of "Mirabeau," a Republican writer in the *National Gazette* subjected deference to a rig-

in 1794 and 1795. The Federalists' frenzied response to Thomas Paine's *Age of Reason* and *Rights of Man* can be followed in Gary B. Nash, "The American Clergy and the French Revolution," *William and Mary Quarterly*, 22 (1965), 392–412.

25. *Farmers' Register*, June 27, 1798.

26. *Independent Gazetteer*, reprinted from the *Pittsburgh Gazette*, July 26, 1794.

orous examination, calling all signs of it "forerunners of monarchy and aristocracy in the United States." This precipitated a discussion of the use of honorifics in general, "reverend" being singled out in particular as "not only antirepublican but absoluely blasphemous." "Citizens" was widely touted as a suitable substitute, but one Federalist wag, noting its sexual designation, proposed replacing citizen with biped. "This title is perfectly simple, it is male or female: it is not aristocratic in origin, and while it accords with truth, it cannot bear the suspicion of flattery."[27] But biped didn't catch on. Philip Freneau, the editor of the first major Republican newspaper, and William Duane, who succeeded to that position, specialized in satirical jibes at the aristocratic pretensions of the Federalists. With circulation of both the *National Gazette* and the *Auora* reaching 1700, the newspaper vendetta against social distinctions was carried into most of the towns of the United States.[28]

What came most sharply into focus in the Republicans' running attack on what they called aristocracy was the fact that the public manners of the new national government reflected the private style of the nation's elite. The decorum, formality, even the secrecy, embodied the mores of those who deliberately distanced themselves from the many, thus creating dissonance between the theory of democracy and its practice. Where Republicans celebrated July 4th at local taverns, Federalists retired to their private homes. The President's weekly levees were drenched with a politeness off-putting to ordinary men and women. "The wrapping up negotiations in mysteries of state, in imitation of the cabinets of despots should be unknown in the clear, manly, and direct expostulation of republican agents," the western Pennsylvania democrats proclaimed.[29]

The political disputes of the 1790s only brought to the surface deeply rooted popular antagonism to elite pretensions, but it was the political implication of such pretensions which gave critics their opening. The Revolution had ob-

27. Hazen, *Contemporary American Opinion of the French Revolution*, pp. 209–16.
28. Clarence L. Brigham, *Journals and Journeymen* (Philadelphia, 1950), pp. 20–21.
29. *Independent Gazetteer*, July 26, 1794.

viously made many Americans peculiarly conscious of class distinctions. In the *Freeman's Journal,* a long letter from a Baltimore correspondent excoriated the drafters of newspaper ads for insinuating little phrases that gave "a plain intimation, if not an absolute assertion, of his or her being in some sense or another WELL BORN." He listed examples: "A gentlemen having about two or three months leisure time would be happy to employ it in transcribing etc.," "Want a place in a store a Young Man of a *good family,*" "To be sold, the time of a servant girl from Germany who says she is of *a very good family.*" "Now what," the writer asked rhetorically, "are their *good families* and *gentility* to the republicans of America? We accomplished the late Revolution without being Well Born (that is, we are descended only from plain laborious ancestors), we have sense enough to become legislators, merchants, farmers and manufacturers without being Well Born; and why, young gentlemen and ladies, cannot you manage our books of accounts, or take care of our stores and kitchens without being *Well Born?*" Another Republican reminded his audience that "neither genius, nor exquisite subtlety of refinement is necessary to the ordinary disquisition of politics."[30]

The controversy in Philadelphia over the licensing of dramatic productions elicited a similar attack on the theater. Beginning sarcastically with reference to "our present state of imaginary republican equality," one writer went on to explain that aristocracy and monarchy depended upon belief in the inherent superiority of one group of men. Plays, he said, by ridiculing "a sneaking subservient tradesman and a dirty blundering Plowman" lead ordinary people to join in the laughter and thereby "learn gradually to despise themselves, whilst the nobleman or the prince is exhibited in all his gaudy trappings, steps into his coach and rolls off into envied grandeur."[31] The social distinctions embedded in

30. *Freeman's Journal,* September 12, 1787; and Tunis Wortman, *A Treatise Concerning Political Enquiry, and the Liberty of the Press* (New York, 1800), p. 65. The recrudescence of aristocratic pretensions among the socially ambitious members of the revolutionary army officer corps is detailed in Charles Royster, *A Revolutionary People at War: The Continental Army and American Character, 1775–1783* (Chapel Hill, 1979).

31. *Freeman's Journal,* April 11, 1784.

penal codes provoked specific democratic reforms as well. William Keteltas, a New York Republican, threw New York City into an uproar in 1795 when he championed the case of two Irish ferrymen who had been arrested for insulting an alderman. Convicted without counsel, without jury, without an opportunity to testify on their own behalf, the ferrymen were sentenced to two months at hard labor and one received twenty-five lashes as well. Claiming that the two had been punished merely "to gratify the pride, ambition and insolence of men in office," Keteltas laid the case before the New York State Assembly which earned him a jail sentence for contempt of the house, but not before the ferrymen's cause had been aired in the newspapers as another example of the oppression of the defenseless poor by the haughty rich.[32]

John Pintard, a New York journalist and businessman, confided to his diary the puzzlement Federalists felt at the peculiar sense of injury evinced by humble folk who had formerly known their place. Worrying about the effect of Republican propaganda on the minds of the people, Pintard confessed that "the spirit of democracy appears to me to be founded in jealously and envy, the most malignant passions of the human heart." He then went on to tell about an incident in which Mrs. Pintard was advising her nurse, a woman described as oppressed with a large family and a worthless drunken husband, "to put some of her children out to service, as a means of lessening her difficulties and disencumbering herself from the charges of clothing and feeding them." Instead of receiving this advice in the friendly light it was intended, the nurse, Pintard wrote in amazement, viewed it "as an insult and immediately exclaimed in a tone of resentment and despair that she believed the government was tending to that pass, when every poor person would have to be the servant of the rich."[33]

32. Young, *Democratic Republicans of New York*, pp. 480–90. Contemporary opinion of the Keteltas affair can be followed in the *New York Journal*, December 26, 30, 1795; February 2, 16, 19, 1796; March 1, 8, 11, 15, 1796.

33. Diary of John Pintard, May 7, 1798, New York Historical Society Collection.

Charles Nisbet, the Scottish-born president of Dickinson College, had a similarly disquieting experience of unintentionally arousing the ire of ordinary men. Hoping to calm the agitated spirits in western Pennsylvania during the Whiskey Rebellion, he delivered a sermon on the text "that ye study to be quiet, and to do your own business, and to work with your own hands, as we commanded you," drawing from Scripture and experience, as his memorialist wrote, "to show that all men were not equally fitted to be Philosophers, Legislators, and Statesmen but that some were intended for working with their hands." His sermon gave such offense—"such doctrine did not suit this side of the Atlantic," one parishioner told him—that it was with great difficulty that a mob was averted from doing damage to Nisbet's house.[34]

It is in the light of these incidents that the exaggerated polemics over aristocracy and monarchy must be interpreted. Few in the 1790s believed that actual titles of nobility would be introduced. What alarmed many ordinary people as well as a distinguished group of upper-class political figures was the Federalist expectation that the new American political institutions would continue to function within the old assumptions about a politically active elite and a deferential, compliant electorate. The underlying issue was unmistakably one about class, for no one had ever questioned the propriety of mere citizens who happened also to be considered gentlemen discussing public measures or bringing pressure to bear upon their legislators. But when ordinary men leapt into the fray of politics they turned them into a fray—a noisy public quarrel. The right of participation could not be extended to the many without changing the style and the substance of republican government. George Washington had hoped that his enormous prestige would bring that great, sober, commonsensical citizenry politicians are always addressing to see the dangers of self-created societies. His censure of them only boomeranged on the Federalists because the majority of Republicans would not be chastened.

34. Samuel Miller, *Memoir of the Rev. Charles Nisbet, D.D.* (New York, 1840), p. 228.

Instead, they carried the dispute to the newspapers, where a new conception of the meaning of popular sovereignty was thrashed out.

The genteel tradition was not exorcized from America, but it was politicized. The Republican creed published in the *National Gazette* and elsewhere made the point well: "I believe," the fourth affirmation read, "that a man who holds his fellow citizens at an awful distance in private life will hold them in contempt if he finds himself placed above them."[35] The class consciousness evident in bitter references to the rich and the well-born did not, however, lead the Republicans to form a party of commoners. They did not take aim at a class of men, but rather at a concept of class—at the belief in inherent, irradicable differences among men. In attacking the elitist assumptions of the Federalists, the Republicans revealed how keenly aware they were that social usages undergirt the distribution of political power. John Adams compared his opponents to those French radicals who panted for equality of persons and property, but this charge was a red herring. Republicans were quite clear about the kinds of equality they panted after: equal political power, equal access to riches, and what J.R. Pole has called "equality of esteem."[36]

Samuel Latham Mitchell's explication of the link between political and economic opportunity typifies the Republican position: "All citizens are acknowledged equal as to their rights, and the only inequality subsisting is that which arises necessarily from office, talents or wealth. But as the road lay open for everyone to aspire to these, it is by the exercise of one or more of his rights that a man acquires these means of influence." Making this process specific, Mitchell went on to trace the career of the landless man who moves to a new area, where he becomes a freeholder. He votes at elections and is eligible for office and naturali-

35. *Kentucky Herald,* December 29, 1795, as cited in Stewart, *Opposition Press,* pp. 495–96.

36. J.R. Pole, *The Pursuit of Equality in American History* (Berkeley, 1978). Charles Royster, *A Revolutionary People at War* (Chapel Hill, 1979), pp. 205–11, offers new evidence of the aspirations for and by an American elite.

zation entitles him to all the rights of citizenship. "Give us universal suffrage," James Cheetham said, was the exclamation of "every honest thinking man." "It is on the principle of equality alone that the liberty of man is founded . . . nor is it likely that revolutions will cease until its establishment be as universal as man."[37]

John Adams's political treatises particularly stirred Republicans because he claimed that inequality was rooted in human nature. His errors, an anonymous critic in Newark's *Centinel of Freedom* said, could be traced to "the misapplication of the histories of other countries to the United States and to that false hypothesis that those who are proud of their wealth, blood or wit, will never give way to fair and equal establishments."[38] The charge of aristocracy and monarchy so common in the polemics of this period is best read as an inflammatory way of saying that the principle of natural equality was being denied. At last the day of reckoning for the rhetoric of the Declaration of Independence had arrived and Republicans went after those who exalted the few with a vengeance.

The brief Indian summer of Federalist ascendency came in 1798 when the French Directory began harassing American shipping and rebuffed the Adams peace mission with the nefarious offers of Messrs. X, Y, and Z. A shift of public opinion away from the pro-French Republicans gave the Federalists a nice majority in Congress. With this opportunity to control political discourse and demonstrate their conception of its proper limits, they passed the Alien and Sedition Laws. Parading a hubris fit for the heroes of tragedy, the Federalists prosecuted every major Republic news-

---

37. Samuel Latham Mitchell, *An Oration, Pronounced Before the Society of Black Friars* (New York, 1793), pp. 20–22; and [James Cheetham], *A Dissertation Concerning Political Equality* (New York, 1800), p. 12.

38. *Centinel of Freedom,* November 23, 1796. See also November 2, 1796, in which the question is raised, "What opinion can a freeman entertain of the love of liberty and political equality possessed by a man who boldly tells the world, that there are different grades and castes in every society, arising from natural causes, and that these grades and castes must have a separate influence and power in the government, in order to preserve the whole: in short, that the turbulence of the common people must be kept within bounds by a hereditary nobility and descendable limited monarchy?"

paper publisher along with more than a dozen other minor journalists and outspoken administration critics. When they used their unfamiliar popularity to silence their opponents, the Republican prophecy of repression was fulfilled. For five years democratic writers had said that the Federalists could not abide free speech; the sedition prosecutions confirmed their predictions. For the next two years the public was treated to a succession of trials in which defendants like Thomas Cooper struggled to prove the truth of such an innocuous statement as that when Mr. Adams entered into office "he was hardly in the infancy of political mistakes." Cooper failed in the attempt and spent six months in prison, a fate suffered by nine other defendants before the voters swept the Republicans into office and the Alien and Sedition Acts were allowed to expire.[39]

It is one of the great ironies of our history that those gentlemen who supported the Constitution because they wanted to remove power from the local level where it was exposed to maniuplation by popular majorities actually created the national forum that made possible the democratization of American politics. Without a national government there would have been no center for that vigorous exercise of authority and display of elite superiority that so alarmed ordinary men. Without a national government there would not have been the nationwide elections which became referenda for the Whiskey Rebellion, Jay's Treaty, the rights of free association, the XYZ Affair and the Adams administration's sedition prosecutions. Without a national government there would not have been the rapid development of mail service, post roads, and newspapers that the Republicans used with such stunning success. In the single decade of the 1790s America's 75 post offices increased to 903; the miles of post roads went from a mere 1,875 to 21,000. The number of newspapers grew correspondingly from less than 100 in 1790 to 250 by 1800. Twenty towns in Pennsylvania, New York, and New Jersey got their first newspaper in these

39. John Davison Lawson, ed., *American State Trials* (St. Louis, Mo., 1914–1936), 10, 785–809. The most thorough coverage of the sedition trials remains James Morton Smith, *Freedom's Fetters* (Ithaca, 1956).

years. Where newspapers were scarce, election broadsides and campaign pamphlets were distributed. The magazine *Port Folio* declared the United States to be "a nation of newspaper readers." Literacy too was exceptionally high among ordinary men. Pierre Samuel Dupont claimed that a large part of the American nation read the Bible while all of the nation "assiduously peruses the newspapers. The fathers read them aloud to their children while the mothers are preparing the breakfast."[40]

Once the democratic societies that promoted much of this literature came under attack, the issue of free speech quickly moved to the foreground of public attention and stayed there for the remainder of the decade. It represented a complex of new and old concerns: the relationship between dignity and authority, the blurred line between public and private realms, and the competence of ordinary people to deliberate on weighty matters of state. More elusive is the passion for political expression that is so marked in these years. Literally hundreds of obscure men took up their pens and scribbled off a tract, a newspaper essay, or a campaign pamphlet. John Beckley, who came about as close to a political hack as the times produced, nonetheless produced a series of essays on the crisis of Jay's Treaty. Dozens of other Republicans are known to us only as the author of a particular piece. This outpouring of writing from ordinary men suggests why even the vigorous prosecutions of the Federalists could not dam the flow of opposition literature.

40. Howard B. Rock, *Artisans of the New Republic: Tradesmen of New York City in the Age of Jefferson* (New York, 1979), pp. 36–40; and Bernard Bailyn et al., eds., *The Great Republic* (Lexington, Ma., 1977), pp. 358–60. No event in public life was every better predicted than the Federalist effort to suppress the popular press established by the Republicans. For contemporary commentary on the relation of a free press to popular participation in government, see Mitchell, *Oration Before the Black Friars*, p. 26; *Independent Gazetteer*, July 30, 1794 and January 21, 1795 ("the freedom of opinion has been in every time and country, the last liberty which the people have been able to wrest from power"); *President II*, pp. 5–6; *Farmers' Register*, June 13, 1794; and [Peck], *Political Wars of Otsego*, pp. 10–14. Republicans' contempt for the Federalists' fears was best expressed on the floor of Congress by Albert Gallatin (*Annals of the Congress*, 8, 1744–45) when he compared the Federalists' hysteria to that of the British at the time of the French Revolution predicting that "we shall . . . soon hear of fictious conspiracies and pop-gun plots."

The Republican organization that triumphed in 1800 was unprecedented. Where previous popular movements had depended upon strong regional ties and pushed the issue of local autonomy, the Republicans created a movement that was national in scope and universal in its ideological appeal. They did it with words—those printed words that had for so long been owned and exchanged by the world's elites. With words in resolutions, toasts, orations, pamphlets, newspapers, and broadsides they took up positions on the French alliance, relations with Great Britain, the excise tax, and the president's conduct of foreign affairs. When this impertinence was construed as a crime, they engaged the nation in debate on the functional meaning of natural rights. With words they formed a democratic network, with words they created loyalties among strangers, with words—often anonymous words—they defied their social superiors, with words they repelled intimidation. And they did this when the only national institution in the country was the federal government and it was in the hands of their opponents. At a time when the American people were geographically spread out, their economy fragmented, their religious affiliations diverse, the Jeffersonians unified ordinary voters through a vision of classlessness. Its intellectual origins were as old as Hobbes's and Locke's social contract theories, but its material base owed much to the recent changes in the Atlantic economy which put a premium on the commodities reaped on American farms. With this substantial underpinning, Jeffersonians could persuade practical men that the only relevant status was that of "the free and independent man." Their utopia was a society of aspirants bound together by a common need to liberate themselves and human nature from the implicit slurs of elite doctrines.

- 4 -

The Principle of Hope

THE FRENCH Revolution had made explicit in the 1790s what had been implicit in the American Revolution: the possibility of shedding the past, shedding, that is, the belief that the past is the principal source of information about human society. Men and women cannot be separated from their experience, but they can be detached from interpretations of that experience. It is this rejection of the past as a repository of wisdom that constitutes the most important element in the ideology of the victorious Jeffersonian Republicans. A very effective litmus test for distinguishing Republicans from Federalists in the 1790s was their reference to the future, whether or not they expected it to be fundamentally different or basically a continuation of the known.[1] It is this orientation, I think, that explains the te-

1. It is this characteristic that in association with their optimism about the future, their emphasis upon private and voluntary associations, and their insistence upon literal political equality and popular participation clearly distinguishes the Jeffersonians from their Federalist opponents. A considerable body of historical scholarship has been built upon the countervailing conviction that the Jeffersonians represent an American version of the English country party. In this interpretation, the Republican and Federalist conflicts represent a replay of the British political wrangles between court and country. See J.G.A. Pocock, *The Machiavellian Moment* (Princeton, 1975), pp. 333–569; Lance Banning, *The Jeffersonian Persuasion* (Ithaca, 1978); John M. Murrin, "The Great Inversion, or Court versus Country: A Comparison of the Revolution Settlements in England (1688–1721) and America (1776–1816)," in Pocock, ed., *Three British Revolutions: 1641, 1688, and 1776* (Princeton, 1980), pp. 414–15; Robert E. Shalhope, "Thomas Jefferson's Republicanism and Antebellum Southern Thought," *Journal of Southern History*, 42 (1976); *idem.*, "Republicanism and Early American Historiography," *William and Mary Quarterly*, 39 (1982); and Rowland Berthoff, "Independence and Attachment, Vir-

nacity with which the Jeffersonians clung to the French alliance through its many perplexing zigzags from right to
left to right again. France's revolution was so precedent-
shattering, so confounding to expectations based upon the
past, that its symbolic importance far outweighed any liabil-
ity incurred through the Reign of Terror or the rise of Na-
poleon.

Americans throughout the revolutionary era had come
to view themselves as a special case. Although James Madison made elaborate studies of ancient confederations in
preparation for the constitutional convention, he argued in
the Virginia ratifying convention that the American situation did not permit useful comparisons. Dozens of other
speakers in the ratification debates echoed this conclusion
as they expatiated upon the novelty of Americans deliberating about their political forms rather than having them
imposed by force or fraud.[2] This self-congratulatory attitude was congenial to the thinking of most public figures
and grew out of a generation of writing about America's
remarkable population growth, its broad suffrage, and the
absence of large numbers of footloose, abjectly poor men
and women such as one found in France or England.[3] The

tue and Interest: From Republican Citizen to Free Enterpriser, 1787–1837," in
Richard L. Bushman et al., eds., *Uprooted Americans: Essays to Honor Oscar Handlin*
(Boston, 1979). Although it is my contention that both country and court thinkers
in the United States went into the Federalist fold, clearly some country figures like
John Randolph, Abraham Yates, and John Taylor became Jeffersonians. Matthew
Lyon's attack on Randolph as reported in the *Annals of the Congress,* 8th Cong.,
February 1, 1805, 1121–26, conveys a sense of the dissimilarity in the conceptual
order of Randolph and mainstream Republicans. Randolph's head, according to
Lyon, was "as full of British contracts and British modes of corruption as ever
Don Quixote's was supposed to have been of chivalry, enchantments, and knight
errantry—a person who seems to think no man can be honest and independent
unless he has inherited lands and negroes, nor is he willing to allow a man to vote
in the people's elections, unless he is a landholder." Jeffersonians like Randolph
are treated at some length in Norman K. Risjord, *The Old Republicans: Southern
Conservatism in the Age of Jefferson* (New York, 1965). Although (p. 3) Risjord says
that the Old Republicans broke with Jefferson because he was not liberal enough
for them, I think it would be more accurate to say "libertarian enough."

2. Peter C. Hoffer, "The Constitutional Crisis and the Rise of a Nationalistic
View of History in America, 1786–1788," *New York History,* 52 (1971), 311–17.

3. As conservative a man as Gouverneur Morris rhapsodized in his diary, "Oh!
my Country, how infinitely preferable that equal Partition of Fortune's Gifts which

rejection of the past that figured prominently in the Republican writings of the 1790s went beyond this earlier, flattering belief in American exceptionalism. It represented a faith in the future that was altogether novel, a future that embraced the entire human race.

Basic to this new faith was a reconceptualization of human nature. The postlapsarian view—"in Adam's fall did sin we all"—was stigmatized, as it had not been before, as a class doctrine. "Whence is it that the doctrine of the equality of man has so long been hidden from the human race?" Phineas Hedges asked an Ulster County July 4th crowd, and proceeded to answer his rhetorical question with a history of repression starting with the Egyptians and ending with Great Britain.[4] Typical of this new approach was Tunis Wortman's "Oration on the Influence of Social Institutions Upon Human Morals and Happiness" given before the Tammany Society in 1796. In one of the most ambitious efforts to reconcile the abilities of ordinary men with the historic proof of their debased condition, the author, a young New York lawyer, grounded his optimism about the future on the malleable nature of the human mind. Wortman developed the familiar enlightenment argument about the baleful influence of autocratic governments and pointed out the conundrum that they condemn people to ignorance and superstition and hence produce the evils that are used to justify their repressiveness. Debasing human character in this way, he said was "the constant and uniform theme of tyrants." The subversive aspects of these statements were not lost on audiences brought up on the Calvinist doctrine of original sin. By connecting the idea of the depravity of man with the venerable rationales for authoritarian institutions, Wortman was clearly flinging down the gauntlet to those Federalist magistrates and ministers who endorsed energetic government. According to him, "excessive energy

you enjoy! Where none are Vassals, none are Lords, but all are Men," *Diary of the French Revolution 1789–1803*, Beatrix Cary Davenport, ed. (New York, 1939), p. 73.

4. Phineas Hedges, *An Oration Delivered Before the Republican Society of Ulster County* (Goshen, N.Y., 1795), p. 3.

in government" accounted for "all those rigid codes of law
that have subverted the natural liberties of mankind." He
concluded his oration by saying that "those who think that
men are naturally vicious and degraded will of consequence
become attached to that form of government which em-
braces the greatest proportion of coercion and restraint."
For other, enlightened men, the popular belief that human
vices and virtues "are part of man's original constitution"
had been shown up as false, Wortman said, because reason
had demonstrated that ugly human qualities should be
traced instead to "the errors and abuses that have at every
period existed in political establishments."[5]

These assertions about the newly discovered capacity of
human beings to develop constructively under conditions of
freedom undermined traditional notions about authority in
several ways. By denying natural inequality they undercut
the old argument that God had created the talented few for
some purpose. Making authoritarian institutions the cause
rather than the consequence of human waywardness turned
the traditional justification for them on its head, while at the
same time the new claims that human beings could take care
of themselves removed the rationale for vigorous government. As James Cheetham crowed, America was "an unan-
swerable confutation of the pestilent doctrines of the advocates of despotic powers, from the days of Robert Filmer to
those of Edmund Burke." The doctrine he had in mind
taught that "a government based upon freedom and equality can have no being but in the imagination."[6]

"The free and independent man," a disgruntled Federalist wrote in his diary, is the Republicans' great idol.
"After finding power to originate in the free and independent man," he went on to comment sardonically, "we have
yet to inquire whether this free and independent man will
voluntarily submit to the restraints which the good of the
community requires of him." Federalists might indeed re-

5. Tunis Wortman, *Oration on the Influence of Social Institution Upon Human
Morals and Happiness* (New York, 1796), pp. 4–7.

6. James Cheetham, *A Dissertation Concerning Political Equality, and the Corpora-
tion of New York* (New York, 1800), p. v.

main skeptical—it was their cohering principle—but Republicans suppressed doubt by making extravagant claims for the unprecedented nature of the times.[7] Eschewing the traditional linkage between past and present, they cultivated in its place a lively connection between present and future. This substitution worked to free political discourse from the concrete imagery of historic references. Because the future is necessarily imaginary public rhetoric gravitated toward those abstract universals that Locke had introduced into politics and Adam Smith into economics.

"Posterity, if not the present age, will view the revolution of the United States as an event the most singular and extraordinary that ever occurred in the annals of human transactions," James Cheetham claimed, while Phineas Hedges told an Ulster County gathering that "the independence of America in all its consequences is one of the most important revolutions in the history of man. The boisterous and precipitate revolutions of Greece and Rome vanish into nothing when compared to the revolution of America." A broadside circulating in Maryland announced that "the genius of universal liberty has been drawn from the pages of philosophy where it has slept for ages, but the doctrine of universal rights has given it a real existence in this and other republics." An anonymous pamphleteer in Philadelphia exulted that American liberty has astounded the world: "A symmetrical fabric arose from the Western wilderness which amazed and confounded the duplicity and iniquity of Europe." Wortman in his oration joined the chorus in affirming that the times were unparalleled: "Moral light has darted its rays upon the world. It has diffused its invigorating influence throughout every department of social life, and exalted the human character to a state of splendid greatness and perfectibility, that no former age has ever yet realized or experienced."[8]

7. [Alexander Graydon], *Memoirs of a Life, Chiefly Passed in Pennsylvania within the Last Sixty Years* (Edinburgh, 1822), p. 426.

8. Cheetham, Dissertation, p. v; Hedges, *Oration*, p. 10; broadside advertising "The American: A Country Gazette," Baltimore, November 19, 1799; *President II. Being Observations on the Late Official Address of George Washington* (Philadelphia, 1796), p. 6; and Wortman, *Oration*, p. 10.

Thomas Paine announced that it was an age of revolution. The Federalist publisher, John Ward Fenno, called it "an age of insurrection," while a country editor conveyed much the same thought when he left standing the headline, "More Revolutions." "American independence," Phineas Hedges maintained, held out hope for "unfettered, unrestrained, progressive improvement" once the people divested themselves of the "errors of representation of property and ceased paying homage to the wealthy." Much was made of the novelty of American institutions. "Representation by election is the very life of a Republican government," wrote a newspaper columnist, going on to claim that "representation equally proportioned according to numbers was never enjoyed in any state, by any people, until the American set the first example." Even Jefferson seemed to be infected with this notion. Writing a friend that the full experiment of a government both democratic and representative had been reserved for America, he declared that "the introduction of this new principle of representative democracy has rendered useless almost everything written before on the structure of government," adding somewhat slyly, "and in a great measure relieves our regret, if the political writings of Aristotle, or of any other antient have been lost." "The moment that the American principle of a representative Government based upon a perfect equality of rights was naturalized in France," formed, according to a writer in Philadelphia's *Independent Gazetteer,* "the most eventful epoch of civil history. Till this period the art of Government had been but the study and benefit of the few to the exclusion and depression of the many; but from this auspicious moment, a new scene has opened on the Theater of human affairs."[9]

Such bombast did more than appeal to the pride of the

9. Thomas Paine, "The Rights of Man" in Philip S. Foner, ed., *The Complete Writings of Thomas Paine* (New York, 1945), I, 4; *Gazette of the United States,* December 18, 1798, as cited in J. Wendell Knox, *Conspiracy in American Politics, 1787–1815* (New York, 1972), p. 124; Hedges, *Oration,* p. 1.; *Centinel of Freedom,* January 4, 1797; Thomas Jefferson to Izaac H. Tiffany, August 26, 1816, in Andrew A. Lipscomb and Albert Ellery Bergh, eds., *The Writings of Thomas Jefferson* (Washington, 1905), XV, 65–66, and *Independent Gazetteer,* January 14, 1975.

men and women living in this extraordinary age. It also set
up a rhetorical dynamic that Republicans used to great effect. The American record in political inventiveness—first
in establishing governments in 1776 and then in refashion-
ing the federal compact eleven years later—supplied concrete evidence of successful, deliberate social action. At the
same time the declarations and preambles featured in the
revolutionary season of constitution-writing popularized the
creed of natural rights. The discernible changes in American institutions made these idealistic affirmations seem like
practical goals to sober, down-to-earth men. Seemingly legitimate expectations were raised. Upon reflection, we can
see that the soft underbelly of any society, at least in ideological terms, is the gap between its shared moral commitments and day-to-day fidelity to those unifying principles.
The commitments are important creators of solidarity, but
high expectations unfulfilled fuel discontent. In normal
times we live with this lapse, albeit with twinges of conscience, but there are occasions when the distance between
promise and performance provides fertile ground for those
bent upon transforming social institutions. As challengers to
those in power in the 1790s, the Republicans took advantage of the shortfall between radical revolutionary rhetoric
and conservative political practices. An earlier vague and
high-flown allusion to equality became for them a literal insistence upon exact numerical voting shares. Equally literal
was their interpretation of the venerable doctrine of popular sovereignty. Literary references to officials as "servants
of the people" were taken seriously, and the ordinary vot-
er's claim to a fair share in office-holding was vigorously
staked out.

The revolutionary spirit in America had unleashed a
cluster of humanitarian hopes that should be differentiated
from the Republicans' reform agenda. The drives for the
manumission and abolition of slavery, for changes in the
states' draconian penal codes, and for public funding for
schools, cut across political persuasions. Federalists were as
active as Republicans in these reform movements which
drew heavily upon religious groups indifferent to politics

altogether. Where the Republicans distinguished themselves was in their single-minded effort to refashion the political institutions of the United States—to liberate, if you will, their idol, "the free and independent man." Liberation for them meant lifting the dead hand of the past and penetrating the time-bound pretensions of a privileged elite. Federalists insisted that American institutions were but improvements upon old forms, particularly those of England. They stressed the continuity of institutional arrangements and of the rationale for them. The Republicans exaggerated the unparalleled novelty of American constitutions and used that novelty as proof of the possibility of dramatic social change. Their interpretation of reality provoked their opponents to argue that social innovations were neither good nor possible, a counterattack that made even more conspicuous the elitist underpinnings of traditional theory.

What clearly animated the Republicans was the principle of hope.[10] But hope, as we well know, comes in many shapes and sizes. There are modest, personal hopes; there are cosmic, transcendental hopes. It takes a collective hope to generate political movements. Only at certain moments are large numbers of people open to a vision of secular change. At these times hope acts as an engine for change because it supplies energy for converting dreams into reality. This is how hope operated in the 1790s.

Republican hopes in fact were fed from many sources. The successful Revolution against England was one such. The foes of religious uniformity took heart from the disestablishment of the Church of England in Virginia. A tribute to the combined efforts of the dissenting Presbyterian and Baptist sects and religious rationalists like Madison and Jefferson, the decade-long struggle involved the mobilization of thousands of ordinary voters. Another lively expression of hope in the 1790s bubbled up from millenarian springs. Jedidiah Peck, for instance, mingled quotations from

10. I have taken this title from Ernst Bloch, *Das Prinzip Hoffnung* (Frankfurt, 1973), which unfortunately has not been translated into English. Bloch's ideas have been treated at length in a special issue of *New German Critique*, no. 9 (1976).

Thomas Paine and predictions of the global spread of representative democracy with references to monarchies as the anti-Christ, the beast, and the literal kingdom of Satan. Imagery from the Book of Revelations was frequently evoked to describe the social order aborning, and evangelical Protestants found nothing incompatible between their piety and the affirmation of the natural and imprescriptible rights of man. Another strong source of hope issued from the fact of scientific achievement. Writers spoke of the recent attainment of "the true principles of political science." One Republican announced that "comparatively society is in political science what infants are respecting knowledge." Another suggested that progressive improvement would enable men "to penetrate into the mysteries of animate and inanimate matter.[11]

The economy nurtured hopes in two complementary ways. The sense of a new commercial age fed into expectations of fundamental change, and the conception of the economy as a natural system with lawlike regularities provided specific answers to the reservations expressed by conservatives. Hardly a Republican gathering disbanded without hearing toasts and resolutions extolling agriculture and trade. "In a free government," as one typical orator explained, "commerce expands her sails; Prompted by a spirit of enterprize and a desire of gain, men venture the dangers of a boisterous ocean in pursuit of new commodities. With wider acquaintance of man the elements of the monk and the barbarian dissolve into the sympathizing heart of a citizen of civilized life." "Legislators of the people," an anonymous writer said, "should never neglect any means of promoting agriculture. It is the basis of the happiness of the people, the strength of empires, the aliment of commerce, and the foundation of manufacturers." In a similarly exclamatory manner, Republican Congressman Edward

11. [Jedidiah Peck], *The Political Wars of Otsego* (Cooperstown, 1796), pp. 10–14; Wortman, *A Treatise Concerning Political Enquiry,* pp. 19–29; Cheetham, *Dissertation,* p. 9; [Isaac Ledyard], *An Essay on Matter* (Philadelphia, 1784); Hedges, *Oration,* p. 12.

Livingston toasted "The Colossus of American freedom—may it bestride the commerce of the world."[12]

As even these celebratory remarks suggest, Republican claims for future economic development were tied to the belief in economic freedom. Alexander Hamilton labeled the idea that commerce might regulate itself a "wild speculative paradox," but Adam Smith's invisible hand was warmly clasped by the Republicans. Jefferson ordered a number of copies of Thomas Cooper's *Political Arithmetic* for distribution as campagin material in 1800.[13] It admirably set forth the reasons for leaving the economy alone. Cooper was a British radical whose enthusiasm for constitutional reform had got him in trouble in England and subsequently landed him in jail in the United States when he became one of the martyrs of the Federalist sedition prosecutions. Although he came from a prominent calico-manufacturing family, he wholeheartedly embraced the American economy of food and fiber exports. Agricultural commodities, he noted, did not depend upon forced markets like the plated candlesticks of Birmingham or velvets from Manchester. "Forced markets" was a euphemism for luxury sales and was meant to provoke an invidious comparison with supplying the staff of life to a hungry world. "If buyers will go to China for teacups," Cooper wrote, "they will come to America for bread." The conclusion he drew from this fact was that Americans needed neither a merchant marine nor a navy and hence should not be taxed for either. As he explained it, "I have no objection to our commerce being carried on by foreign capital but the contrary, for I think our domestic capital can be much better employed, but I have great ob-

12. *Ibid.*, p. 11; *Farmers Register*, May 23, 1798; and *Whitestown Gazette*, October 31, 1797, as cited in Alfred F. Young, *The Democratic Republicans of New York* (Chapel Hill, 1967), p. 581. See also [Alexander James Dallas], *Features of Mr. Jay's Treaty* (Philadelphia, 1795), pp. 21–22.

13. *Continentalist No. V*, April, 1782 in Harold C. Syrett, ed., *The Papers of Alexander Hamilton* (New York, 1962), III, 76; and Dumas Malone, *The Public Life of Thomas Cooper, 1783–1839* (New Haven, 1925), pp. 101, 190–91. The different commitment to "the new order versus the old" which surfaced in Hamilton and Jefferson's commercial policies was pointed out by Merrill Peterson in his review of the eighteenth and nineteenth volumes of *The Papers of Thomas Jefferson, William and Mary Quarterly*, 32 (1975), 656–58.

jections to the interest of the whole nation being sacrificed, our citizens and our property wasted by wars and taxes." The taxes raised to build a navy, which was the issue he was addressing, would not fall on the merchants, he maintained, but upon "the farmer, the mechanic, the labourer. They and they alone pay." In an economy in which the bulk of the white laboring force was self-employed the issue of taxes was very much akin to that of wages in our day. Lower taxes left more in the hands of the agricultural producers whose investments held out hope of raising crop yields. "The whole capital spent on agricultural improvements is gain to the community, the whole of the spur to industry is at home whereas the capital of the merchant is beneficial directly to himself alone." Driving home his point, Cooper concluded: "The merchants form a small class; the consumers form the nation."[14]

In the event, Jefferson as president did protect the American carrying trade on the grounds that the Constitution guaranteed such protection, but Cooper's basic program stated in dozens of other Republican tracts prevailed as Jeffersonian policy. "Prohibit nothing," Cooper said, "but protect no speculation, no investment of capital at an expense beyond its national value." Cut the cost of government, eliminate direct taxes, and spend customs revenue on domestic investment was his message or, as he put it, "improve your roads, clear your rivers, cut your canals, erect your bridges, facilitate intercourse, establish schools and colleges, diffuse knowledge of all kinds."[15]

By and large the men who figured out how to cut better canals and facilitate commercial intercourse were Republicans, and they mingled their gifts for practical invention with literary tributes to the new age of improvements. Thomas Paine, who traveled from revolution to revolution with a valise filled with designs for an improved iron bridge, was the prototype for a score of others. Joel Barlow wrote poetry, philosophical tracts, and pamphlets on internal improvements while he went about Europe hawking land in

14. Thomas Cooper, *Political Essays* (Philadelphia, 1800), pp. 50, 34, 43.
15. *Ibid.*, p. 50.

America's West. Jefferson and Madison once proposed buying a male merino sheep for every county in Virginia. Robert Fulton patented a machine for sawing marble, one for spinning flax, and another for twisting hemp into rope. He also developed the submarine, a steam engine, and a torpedo boat for which he is remembered. Less well known are his political publications, among them an essay "to the Friends of Mankind" which begins by announcing that the interests of men and nature in all countries is universally the same: to wit, "to live in peace and Cultivate the material enjoyments of life." Nothing is truly political and honorable, he went on to explain, but a studious cultivation of the mental and corporeal powers and "a free circulation of the whole produce of Genious and labour." Among other things that fall to the duty of a good Republican, Fulton concluded, was to teach youth just ideas of individual and natural rights and not to teach them that "particular men are their Superiors" or that it is good "to resign their rights on earth in order to gain possession of heaven."[16]

Because so much has been made of the Puritan work ethic in America, it is worth pointing out that the Republicans did not extol those pristine virtues of thrift and frugality. What opened before their eyes was the prospect of the widespread enjoyment of comforts. Indeed, the word comfort sprang into use in these years. Luxuries conjured up an aristocratic economy of elite consumption and plebian toil while necessities brought to mind the penury of age-old limits. Comforts, on the other hand, could be generally aimed at and enjoyed without harm to others. In 1785, when Jefferson and Adams were both in Europe negotiating commercial treaties for the United States, Jefferson actually corrected Adams' draft treaty with Spain, by substituting "comforts" for "necessaries." Workers should have such an equivalent for their labor "as to enable them to live

16. Christine M. Lizanich, " 'The March of this Government': Joel Barlow's Unwritten History of the United States," *William and Mary Quarterly,* 33 (1976); and Robert Fulton, "Address to the Friends of Mankind on the Advantages of Free Trade and the Benefits of an Internal Navigation," New York Historical Society, pp. 24, 28–29.

with comfort," Republican George Logan wrote. An anonymous Republican hailed the United States as "this land of comfort, where, blessed with health, and being industrious, no one needs despair of a comfortable livelihood at least." The Democratic Society of Philadelphia called for the promotion of necessary manufacturers as long as they were "consistent with an economy of full employment and comfortable support for all American citizens."[17] Nor were Republican editors, even those in rural communities, reluctant to dazzle their readers with images of ever-increasing wealth. "Industry," one wrote, "secures the enjoyment of health, strength, and happiness. Under its influence, nature new decks herself in the gayest attire . . . cities rise, forests are transformed into fleets. Men visit their fellow men, and the necessities of one clime are supplied by the superfluities of another. Increasing luxury gives spring to invention." "Agriculture where territory is not wanting is the hand-maid of opulence," wrote another. Thus did the age of limits yield in the imagination to a vision of prosperity, and it did so long before the steam engine and the dynamo disclosed their wonderful powers.[18]

From the Republican *New York Journal* came the endorsement of agriculture as the parent of commerce: "Both together form the great sources from which the wants of individuals are supplied." Despite these panegyrics to industry, it was moderate toil the Republicans aimed for in apparent conformity to American work habits. According to the Duc de La Rochefoucauld, who traveled extensively through the Northern countryside in 1795 and 1796, nonchalance was the most characteristic American trait. Not even on the frontier, he said, did farmers work more than four days a week. "Necesary unremitting labour is a form of des-

17. Thomas Jefferson to John Adams, November 27, 1783, in Lester J. Cappon, ed., *The Adams-Jefferson Letters* (Chapel Hill, 1959), I, 103. See also Joyce Appleby, "Commercial Farming and the 'Agrarian Myth' in the Early Republic," *Journal of American History*, 68 (1982); George Logan, *An Address on the Natural and Social Order* (Philadelphia, 1790), p. 10; *Centinel of Freedom*, November 23, 1796; and "Minutes of the Democratic Society of Pennsylvania," Historical Society of Pennsylvania, p. 74.

18. *Farmers Register*, May 16, 1798; *New York Journal*, April 13, 1785.

potism," according to Cooper. Speaking to one another as fellow human beings, the Republicans abandoned that didacticism that figured so prominently in Federalist social commentary.[19] The hope of a widely diffused prosperity also colored Republican writings on competition. "A liberal mind cannot for a moment harbour the idea that every new artisan is a base plotter of the destruction of his competitor," the Republican editors of *The Farmers Register* charged, going on to justify their starting a second country newspaper on the grounds that "it is only by competition that a town or city can flourish. The united efforts of rival artisans give energy to trade; the public becomes better served and places gradually rise in importance with the celebrity of their manufacturers," a position they concluded, so self-evident that it needed no illustration.[20]

At the most general level, the Republicans' expectation of a sustained prosperity based upon an ever-expanding global exchange of goods undercut the Federalist rationale for energetic government. It was no longer needed to protect the weak from the strong, the hungry from the hoarders, the survival of the whole from the selfish acts of the few. An increased level of productivity had solved that ancient problem. Nor in Republican thinking was government needed to direct economic activities to secure a larger share of a finite pie in an age of commercial expansion. This was what the English example offered and the Republicans feared. As one newspaper writer noted, Great Britain had enjoyed a long period of economic growth, but "the body of the British nation live in a state of abject dependence upon the potent few. The hard earned wages are wrung from the hands of the laboring part of the community" to support the government and pay the interest on a national debt that only grows larger. Here is a critique of the British funded debt that owes nothing to the classical republican

19. *New York Journal,* May 11, 1786; Duc de La Rochefoucauld-Liancourt, *Voyages,* as cited in David J. Brandenburg, "A French Aristocrat Looks at American Farming," *Agricultural History,* 32 (1958), p. 161; and Cooper, *Political Essays,* p. 83.

20. *Farmers Register,* April 18, 1798.

obsession with political corruption.[21] The Republicans interpreted the mercantilist goals of national wealth and power
as parts of another scheme of the few to wrest natural and
equal rights from the many. A similar reinterpretation of
the threat of luxuries also came from Republican pens.

Moralists had long inveighed against luxuries, seeing in
them but the tip of the iceberg of self-indulgence. An old
staple in the Sunday fare of sermons, such indictments of
luxury were frequently but thinly veiled attacks on social
mobility. Sharing the upper-class attitudes of their substantial parishioners, many American ministers viewed the popular consumption of such things as imported fabrics as leading to a dangerous blurring of class lines. Jeffersonians also
attacked luxuries, but from a very different perspective.
Madison developed their line of attack in a series of articles
for the *National Gazette*. Silverplated candlesticks and printed
velvets, as Cooper had said, required forced markets, that is
to say, artificial tastes. According to Madison, the making of
luxuries skewed manufacturing toward the pocketbooks of
the wealthy few, leaving the economy's productive base vul-
nerable to changes in fashion while at the same time creating the hordes of dependent factory operatives who turned
out the lace ruffles and silver knee buckles for the rich. Far
better the Republican argument went, to promote the production of grains and raw materials, which served the interests of ordinary people around the world and depended
upon no government favors for its promotion, no body of
experts for its dextrous management.[22]

The passionate party warfare of the 1790s did not determine whether or not America's economy would be capi-
talistic. That had already been decided long ago with the
integration of the colonies into the great Atlantic trade. Nor
did the contest between the Federalists and Republicans resemble a replay of the earlier colonial division between conservatives and innovators over such things as paper money

21. *Independent Gazetteer*, January 28, 1795.
22. *National Gazette*, March 22, March 29, February 20, 1792, as published in
Gaillard Hunt, ed., *The Writings of James Madison* (New York, 1904), vol. 6, 99–
105, 93–95.

and regulated markets, for both the Republican and Federalist parties were dominated by modernists—men committed to economic change. Rather, the fight was over the social and political context in which this change was to take place. Would the traditional division between the few and the many persist? Would the nation's economic development be directed from the center through the government's fiscal and banking policies? Would those in authority continue to be protected through laws and public usages promoting deference? The natural harmony of autonomous individuals freely exerting themselves to take care of their own interests while expanding the range of free exchange and free inquiry was the liberating alternative Republicans juxtaposed to the Federalists' expectations of orderly growth within venerable social limits. They celebrated work not for its glorification of God but rather for its contribution to human producitivty and knowledge. In place of virtue, they extolled the independence of individuals and the voluntary cooperation of private persons.[23]

In championing the rapid development of Western lands and the worldwide trade in American farm surpluses the Republicans were actually far more economically oriented than the Federalists. As most of Hamilton's biographers have noted, his overriding interests were political. Recent studies have stressed the limitations even to his enthusiasm for manufacturing. However much he may have entertained the idea of making America self-sufficient, he would in fact let nothing interfere with the flow of English trade, which brought in the revenue that serviced the national debt. The speculations that his policies made possible had very little to do with the productive ideal that animated the Republicans. The Louisiana Purchase, far from firing his imagination with dreams of American abundance, only caused him to worry that Americans would move beyond the coercive power of the state. Not sharing Hamilton's con-

23. Wortman, *Oration*, p. 18; Cheetham, *Dissertation*, p. 43; and Logan, *Five Letters, Addressed to the Yeomanry of the United States* (Philadelphia, 1792), p. 28. See also Edward Countryman, *A People in Revolution* (Baltimore, 1981), pp. 294–95; and Young, *Democratic Republicans of New York*, p. 581.

ventional pessimism, Jefferson saw enough free land "for our descendants to the hundredth and thousandth generation."[24] That promise let loose a flood of ingenious designs for improvements and inventions. Contemplating America's cornucopian future dispelled ancient worries about overpopulation and famine.

Economic theory as distinct from economic prospects played an even more direct role in republican ideology. A contrast with classical republican theory will help make the point. Classical republicanism taught that a carefully constructed constitution balancing the forces in society alone held out hope for checking the lust for power and selfish drives of human beings. Government was the artifice—the celebrated achievement—by which men might escape what J.G.A. Pocock has called the terrors of history, that stream of irrational events which repeatedly engulfed men and nations.[25] The conception of the economy as a natural and orderly system invisibly producing social harmony directly challenged this older wisdom and undermined the elaborate rationale for authoritarian institutions. American receptivity to this message can be traced at least as far back as 1776 when Thomas Paine attacked the theoretical underpinnings for Britain's mixed monarchy and bottomed America's right to independence on John Locke's social contract.[26] Government in this view did not embody the civilized goals of the society, nor as in Aristotle's *Politics* did it create the arena where the noblest men might practice civic virtue. Completely reversing the classical order, natural

24. Frederick C. Prescott, ed., *Alexander Hamilton and Thomas Jefferson* (New York, 1934), p. xxxiv; and John R. Nelson, Jr., "Alexander Hamilton and American Manufacturing: A Reexamination," *Journal of American History*, 66 (1979). Jefferson's interest in the technological aspects of economic development was manifested not only in his well-known passion for agricultural improvement, but in industrial inventiveness as well. He possessed a model of the Arkwright machinery (Julian P. Boyd et al., eds., *The Papers of Thomas Jefferson* [Princeton, 1950–], vol. 18, 123n.) and was an early admirer of Eli Whitney, as can be seen through his letter to James Monroe, November 14, 1801, in Paul Leicester Ford, ed., *The Writings of Thomas Jefferson* (New York, 1892–1899), vol. 8, 101–02.

25. J.G.A. Pocock, *The Machiavellian Moment* (Princeton, 1975), viii, p. 458–59.

26. Paine, "Common Sense," in Foner, ed., *Writings of Paine*, vol. I, 8–9.

rights philosophers placed the personal ahead of the public. The natural and voluntary associations of men in society, moreover, reduced the dangers from external threats and internal fragmentation—those untoward invasions and civil wars that filled the pages of ancient history. We get a sense of the application of this new perspective from the western Pennsylvania Republican leader, William Findley, who compared the moral obligation one felt toward repaying a private debt to the amoral willingness to evade taxation. Virtue had lost its public character and attached itself instead to the private rectitude essential to a system of individual bargains. The instrumental attitude toward government implicit in Locke's *Second Treatise* was made explicit by such Jeffersonians as James Cheetham who reminded his readers that the security of life, liberty, and property was the only reason for entering civil society and hence the punishment of offenses against violators of it the major task of government.[27]

Even when Republicans seemed to be talking about the traditional concept of civic virtue the alchemy of material improvement produced gold from the mercury of self-interest. Thus Tunis Wortman in his Tammany speech spoke of a new era devoid of luxury, wealth, and sumptuous dissipation. His reader is entitled to think, "aha, here we are with classical republican ideals of restraint," but instead Wortman went on to describe how a generous emulation would promote economic growth without degenerating into jealousy or envy. "Agriculture and manufacturers will flourish; commerce, unrestrained by treaties and unshackled by partial provisions will become as extensive as the wants and intercourse of nations," Wortman explained, noting that since our interests and our virtue coincide, it was a dangerous error in the present system to place them at variance. Jefferson later expressed the same opinion more emphatically when he told the famous French economist, J.B. Say, "So invariably do the laws of nature create our duties and interests, that when they seem to be at variance, we ought

27. William Findley, *History of the Insurrection in the Four Western Counties of Pennsylvania* (Philadelphia, 1796); and Cheetham, *Dissertation,* p. 23.

to suspect some fallacy in our reasoning." Nature, it seemed, had resolved the age-old tension between individual self-interest and the welfare of the community, making it possible to believe, as Jefferson did, that "the rights of the whole can be no more than the sum of the rights of individuals."[28]

The old formulation had said that only some people were capable of rational behavior and that they should be entrusted with authority to direct others. The modern concept of self-interest gave to all men the capacity for rational decisions directed to personal ends. Conservatives acknowledged the growth of self-interested actions, but in an elegiac spirit. Jeffersonian Republicans seized upon the liberating potential in this new conception of human nature and invested self-interest with moral value. Self-interest—reconceived—turned out to be a mighty leveller, raising ordinary people to the level of competence and autonomy while reducing the rich, the able, and the well-born to equality. The political relevance of elite talents had diminished considerably, for if interestedness dominated all human beings, the superior intellect, education, and refinement of the few was unavailable to the public, as Madison pointed out in his famous *Tenth Federalist*. Limiting the scope of government, therefore, limited the capacity of special interests to interfere with that natural society created by human wants and the uniting, as Paine said, of our affections. It was a point Madison alluded to when he compared most important acts of legislation to judicial determinations and called to mind that no man was allowed to be a judge in his own cause. The very nature of economic development had changed the character of political authority and called into question the disinterestedness of office holders.

The tendency to conceive of social life in naturalistic terms was powerful on both sides of the Atlantic. Indeed, it undergirds the whole intellectual enterprise of the social sciences. But the different circumstances of America and England made a vast difference in what science taught. The bumper crops of babies that began in Europe in the mid-

28. Wortman, *Oration*, p. 18; and Jefferson to Say, February 1, 1804, in Lipscomb and Bergh, eds., *Writings of Jefferson*, vol. 11, 2–3.

eighteenth century furnished the Reverend Thomas Robert Malthus with the grim statistics he fashioned into his famous population theory in 1798. Malthus was apparently responding somewhat maliciously to his father's belief in automatic progress when he insisted that human reproduction would always outstrip the capacity of men and women to produce food. In fact, his theory of inevitable limits to human prosperity were out of date at the time he wrote, but that is something which scholars have just recently demonstrated.[29] For contemporaries the *Essay on Population* provided a scientific explanation for the inexorable misery of the poor. When joined to David Ricardo's ideas about the distribution of income, Malthus's account of growth created a field day for pessimists. With population growth, societies would be forced to till more land to feed the people. Since the best land was already under cultivation, poor land would be brought under the plow. With each increment of inferior land brought into production the rents on better land would increase and the annual returns to landlords be augmented, spreading ever wider the gap between the established and the marginal. These theories of Malthus and Ricardo were cast in the language once reserved for the physical sciences, thus enhancing the impression that society, like the natural world, was subject to the grim rule of cause and effect.

But consider now the American situation. The same population pressure in Europe had raised the price of food and the incentive of higher grain prices had encouraged American farmers to plan for ever-larger surpluses. Jefferson airily dismissed Malthusian fears by claiming that harvests in the United States increased "geometrically with our laborers" enabling Americans to "nourish the now perishing births of Europe, who in return would manufacture and send us in exchange our clothes and other comforts."[30] In-

29. E.A. Wrigley and R.S. Schofield, *The Population History of England 1541–1871* (London, 1981); and Thomas Sowell, "Malthus and the Utilitarians," *Canadian Journal of Economics*, 28 (1962).

30. Jefferson to Say, February 1, 1804, in Lipscomb and Bergh, eds., *Writings of Jefferson*, Vol. 11, 1–3. See also Joyce Appleby, "What is Still American in the Political Philosophy of Thomas Jefferson," *William and Mary Quarterly*, 39 (1982),

stead of moving on to marginal land, Americans were cultivating acres in western Pennsylvania, New York, Maryland, and Virginia, where the soil was so rich that a preliminary crop of corn had to be planted to bring down the fertility or the wheat shafts would bolt. And beyond these new tracts beckoned the uncultivated lands of the Ohio River Valley. The American situation stood Ricardo's iron law of rents and wages on its head, for the more fertile land of the West drove down existing land prices in the rural East. Population growth was pushing Americans onto the best farmland. The small farmer taking up new land had an unparalleled opportunity to capitalize his and his family's labor, since the cleared land of new settlements enjoyed the most consistent rise in value. The prosperity that began in 1789 affected all but the most destitute in the United States. Western lands drew off wage earners from both rural and urban areas, and wages rose as the work force grew smaller. It was a relationship well understood by the Republicans in Congress who voted to reduce the minimum size of land purchases, extend credit to buyers, and place land offices in the areas where ordinary men and women lived. Nor were the benefits confined to farmers. "As yet our manufacturers are as much at their ease, as independent and moral as our agricultural inhabitants," Jefferson explained in a letter in 1805, and "they will continue so as long as there are vacant lands for them to resort to; because whenever it shall be attempted by the other classes to reduce them to the minimum of subsistence, they will quit their trades and go to labouring the earth."[31]

In so thoroughly embracing the liberal position on private property and economic freedom, the Jeffersonians

295–96; and Merrill Peterson, *Thomas Jefferson and the New Nation* (New York, 1970), pp. 771–73.

31. Murray R. Benedict, *Farm Politics of the United States, 1790–1950* (New York, 1953), pp. 12–15; John G. Clark, *The Grain Trade in the Old Northwest* (Urbana, 1966), pp. 2–3; Stanley Lebergott, "Changes in Unemployment 1800–1960," *Journal of Economic History,* 17 (1957); Rudolph Bell, *Party and Faction in American Politics* (Westport, Ct., 1973), pp. 85–89; Billy G. Smith, "Material Lives of Laboring Philadelphians, 1750 to 1800," *William and Mary Quarterly,* 38 (1981), 190; and Thomas Jefferson to Mr. Lithson, January 4, 1805, in Ford, ed., *Writings of Jefferson,* vol. 11, 55.

seemed unable to envision a day when the free exercise of men's wealth-creating talents would produce its own class-divided society. Marx's statement that men and women can only solve the problems history sets before them comes to mind. The prospect of social advance through the personal exertions of individual men in an environment of freedom overcame all doubts. "When we enjoy liberty and are sure of its continuance," Nathaniel Niles wrote, "we feel that our persons and properties are safely guarded and this excites to industry which tends to a competency of wealth." Hugh Henry Brackenridge conjured up the alternative when he described the chagrin and dissatisfaction men felt when they saw others pushed ahead of them because of sudden gain from speculation or unearned privilege. "The Yeomanry of America," George Logan maintained, "only desire what they have a right to demand—a free unrestricted sale for the produce of their own industry and not to have the sacred rights of mankind violated in their persons by arbitrary laws, prohibiting them from deriving all the advantages they can from every part of the produce of their farms." [32]

To Benjamin Rush the natural distinctions of rank as opposed to unnatural privileges were the consequence of "industry and capacity, and above all, commerce." Inequality in the presence of opportunity was a stimulus to others and a reward to the meritorious. Jefferson, who once spoke of having developed a system "by which every fibre of antient or future aristocracy would be eradicated," saw no contradiction in unequal inheritance. "To take from one, because it is thought his own industry and that of his fathers had acquired too much," he wrote near the end of his life, "in order to spare to others who, or whose father have not exercised equal industry and skill, is to violate arbitrarily the first principle of association, the guarantee to everyone a free exercise of his industry and the fruits acquired by it." [33] Natural law in the midst of American abundance

32. Nathaniel Niles, *Two Discourses on Liberty* (Newbury-Port, 1774), p. 22; Hugh Henry Brackenridge, *Modern Chivalry* (Philadelphia, 1793), pp. 47–48; and Logan, *Five Letters*, p. 28. See also *General Advertiser*, June 12, 1793.

33. Dagobert Runes, ed., *Selected Writings of Benjamin Rush* (New York, 1947), pp. 62–63; Julian P. Boyd et al., eds., *The Papers of Thomas Jefferson* (Princeton,

conferred great privileges on ordinary men. With such bounty there seemed no reason to fear the concentration of earned wealth. Freedom no longer appeared as a formal right as in the Magna Carta but rather as a condition for human fulfillment. The presumed naturalness of individuals exerting themselves in their own behalf undercut the paternalism that had so long dominated the relations between the people and their leaders.

It would be a mistake, however, to conclude with the Jeffersonians that in banishing the political distinction between the few and the many and invoking the rights of all men they were in fact dealing with universal truths. In fact their conception of an unvarying, uniform human nature was an intellectual construction of the modernizing nations of the West. It was no less a cultural artifact than the ancient view of the human essence lodged in the four humors or the Puritan description of men and women as the erring children of Adam and Eve. Even in their own day, the rhetoric of the Republicans ignored women, usually excluded slaves, and denied the Native Americans the right to be different. Living cheek by jowl with the Indians—many of them still on ancestral lands—Americans had to confront the inconsistency between their depiction of a universal human nature and the behavior of their neighbors. They resolved the question by placing the onus of deviation upon the Indians. Brackenridge put the case for Republican natural rights with simplicity: "I consider the earth as given to man in common and each should use his share, so as not to exclude others, and should be restricted to that mode of using it, which is most favorable to the support of the greatest number, and consequently productive of the greatest sum of happiness; that is, the cultivation of the soil. I pay little regard, therefore," he said, "to any right which is not founded in agricultural occupancy." Indian land claims he compared to those of children who say it is mine "because I first saw it." Referring to the natural law which gave the earth to men to make fruitful, Brackenridge summarized the liberals' position: "the municipal law binds as citizens,

1950–), vol. 2, 308; and Thomas Jefferson to Joseph Milligan, April 6, 1816, in Lipscomb and Bergh, eds., *Writings of Jefferson*, vol. 14, 466.

the law of nations as societies, but the law of nature as men."[34]

The most glaring contradiction in the Republicans' popular creed was the existence of slavery within the United States, and the Revolution had stirred the American conscience on this issue. North and South, men and women had formed societies to promote manumission, abolition, and black education. By the end of the eighteenth century every Northern state had adopted some form of emancipation. The Mason-Dixon line ceased then to be the surveyors' boundary between Pennsylvania and Maryland and took on its symbolic reference to the division between freedom and slavery. The abolitionist sentiment that had driven slavery fom the North in the 1790s was not monopolized by the Jeffersonians, although Alfred Young is surely right to attribute antislavery opinions among mechanics and tradesmen to "the new egalitarianism."[35] What was vital to the success of the Republicans was not abolition but rather their being able to divorce slavery from their social vision. By focussing upon the prosperity and productivity of a voluntarily integrated economy of free men laboring in their own interest, they freed themselves of the incubus of human bondage. With their emphasis upon the cultivation of food crops on family farms, they were able to retain the moral underpinnings necessary for their dream of a new social order. The importance of sidestepping the slave issue should not be underestimated, for it ran counter to the expectations of most astute observers at the time. Fisher Ames's views are typical. Riveting his attention on the planters of the Southern elite, Ames envisioned sectional differences following the fault line of Messrs. Mason and Dixon. The middle states and New England, he predicted, would come together in a national coalition arrayed against the slave South.[36] Instead, the Jeffersonian opposition welded to-

34. Brackenridge, *Gazette Publications* (Carlisle, 1806; originally published in 1792), pp. 94, 103.

35. Young, *Democratic Republicans of New York*, p. 529.

36. Seth Ames, ed., *Works of Fisher Ames* (Boston, 1854), vol. 1, 101–06. The country cast of Ames's thinking is explored in John W. Malsberger, "The Political Thought of Fisher Ames," *Journal of the Early Republic*, 2 (1982). See also *Columbian*

gether voters from the middle states and the South, leaving New England in political and spiritual isolation.[37]

Jefferson's victory was accompanied by handsome majorities in both Houses of Congress and triumphs in the elections of eleven of the sixteen states. It was sweeping and enduring. Not only did the Republicans control the federal government for the next quarter century, but Federalism as a political force was confined to New England and Delaware. In office, the Jeffersonians carried out their mandate with remarkable fidelity. Direct taxes were repealed, the national debt was quickly retired, revenues were applied to internal improvements, and the size of the federal government was scaled down despite the enlargement of national territory. International free trade was pursued with a vengeance and land sales jumped astronomically. Up-and-coming Federalists were eliminated from the federal civil service, and the rusticity of the new capital at Washington replaced the elegance of Philadelphia.[38] The strict constructionist interpretation of the Constitution that Jefferson failed to impose upon President Washington could now guide him in the presidency. Jefferson referred to the election of 1800

Centinel, May 10, 1794, in which a Federalist author asserted that "One word will serve as a key to all cyphers of the southern faction . . . They hate Britain more than they dread war." In emphasizing the Southern origins of the Republican leaders Federalists clearly failed to perceive their success in building a party base outside the South.

37. The historic origins of this isolation were rooted in both religion and the events of the preceding half century as Nathan O. Hatch has shown in *The Sacred Cause of Liberty: Republican Thought and the Millennium in Revolutionary New England* (New Haven, 1977). The ideological differences manifest in South Carolina politics are discussed in Kenneth S. Greenberg, "Representation and Isolation of South Carolina, 1776–1860," *Journal of American History,* 64 (1977).

38. Drew McCoy, *The Elusive Republic* (Chapel Hill, 1980), p. 250; Carl E. Prince, "The Passing of the Aristocracy: Jefferson's Removal of the Federalists, 1801–1805," *Journal of American History,* 67 (1970), 573–75; Noble Cunningham, Jr., *The Process of Government under Jefferson* (Princeton, 1978), pp. 107, 320–31; Gerald Stourzh, *Alexander Hamilton and the Idea of Republican Government,* Stanford, 1970, p. 193; and Morton Borden, review of Forrest McDonald, *Presidency of Thomas Jefferson,* in *Reviews in American History,* 5 (1977). This recent research, which emphasizes the differences between Federalist and Jeffersonian policies and practices, should lay the ghost of the interpretation offered in Henry Adams, *The History of the United States During the Administration of Jefferson and Madison* (New York, 1889–91), that the Jeffersonians in power "outfederalized" the Federalists.

as a revolution. Historians and political scientists, mindful
of the uncertainty of transferring power, have considered it
a revolution because one party yielded to another in a
peaceful change of the reins of government. Contemporaries saw it differently. The revolution came from the defeat
of aristocratic values in American politics. Writing a generation after the event, Jefferson underscored this point: "The
cherishment of the people then was our principle, the fear
and distrust of them, that of the other party."[39]

What Jefferson's comment fails to note is the fact that
it was the people—ordinary men, political parvenus, outsiders, interlopers, mere voters without office—who created
the turmoil, defined the issues, formed the clubs, manned
the demonstrations, arranged the July 4th celebrations, and
filled the newspaper columns with the rhetoric of Republicanism. They made him President, and the structural loose-
ness of American society served them well in their en-
deavors. Their social superiors did not control them as a
class of employers but rather as public officials and arbiters
of taste. It was in these capacities that the *hoi polloi* challenged and unseated the Federalist elite. Against the cen-
tralizing power of the national government they pitted the
unifying force of liberal Republicanism, and in doing so they
endowed American capitalism with the moral force of their
vision of a social order of free and independent men. The
vision itself was grounded in the particular promise of prosperity held out to Americans at the end of the eighteenth
century. Sound judgements of what was possible at that time
gave substance to exuberant hopes for a qualitatively different future.

If we attend to both the material circumstances and the
ideas those circumstances supported we can perhaps see the
Jeffersonian Republicans whole. Then we will not be
tempted with the Progressives to view them romantically as
agrarian democrats, or to give in to the disappointment of
consensus historians, who discovered in both Federalists and

39. Jefferson to William Johnson, June 12, 1823, in Ford, ed., *Writings of
Jefferson*, vol. 10, 227. For Madison's echo of this statement, see Gaillard Hunt, ed.,
The Writings of James Madison (New York, 1904), vol. 9, 135.

Republicans alike a commitment to the economic values that made America "a democracy of cupidity" rather than one of fraternity.[40] To study the exact nature of the capitalist underpinnings of our nation's first popular political movement, formed at the turn of the nineteenth century, is also to find a more usable past, for it teaches us that we at the turn of the twenty-first century must look elsewhere for our principle of hope.

40. The phrase belongs to Richard Hofstadter.

Index

INDEX